THE BOOK OF RISK

THE BOOK OF RISK

DAN BORGE

John Wiley & Sons, Inc.

New York • Chichester • Weinheim • Brisbane • Singapore • Toronto

Published by John Wiley & Sons, Inc.
Published simultaneously in Canada.

This publication is designed to provide accurate and authoritative information in regard to the subject matter covered. It is sold with the understanding that the publisher is not engaged in rendering professional services. If professional advice or other expert assistance is required, the services of a competent professional person should be sought.

Library of Congress Cataloging-in-Publication Data:

Borge, Dan.
    The book of risk / by Dan Borge.
        p. cm.
    Includes bibliographical references.
    ISBN 0-471-32378-0 (cloth : alk. paper)
    1. Risk management. 2. Risk assessment. 3. Risk-taking (Psychology) I. Title.

HD61.B647 2001
658.15′5—dc21   2001017503

Printed in the United States of America.

10 9 8 7 6 5 4 3 2 1

Dedicated to my daughter,
Caroline Borge

PREFACE

This is not a risk management textbook. A textbook would require more rigor and detail than either you or I could stomach. There are already many excellent sources available on risk management that meet that need. Nor is this a How-to-Risk-Manage-to-Success-in-Ten-Easy-Steps book. I don't believe that either risk management or success is reducible to simplistic rules or recipes that anyone can follow. I do believe, however, that there are general principles of risk management and that if you are aware of them, you have a head start in making better decisions.

What I have tried to do here is put down on paper some thoughts and examples that will pique your interest in risk management, even if you think that you know nothing about it and could care less. If you trust me for a few pages, you may find it to be a subject worth thinking about and arguing about, not only for its intellectual interest, but for its practical value in your professional or personal life.

I will put you in the driver's seat. You will be the decision maker as we explore different ways to confront and manage risks. Risk management is for decision makers and if you view it from that perspective, you will have a much better chance of appreciating its power. I will be your guide, advisor, and coach.

Let's get started.

DAN BORGE

Clinton Corners, New York
March 2001

CONTENTS

THE BOOK OF RISK

Chapter 1

WHAT IS RISK MANAGEMENT AND WHY SHOULD YOU CARE?

The term "risk management" is loaded with connotations of caution and timidity, carrying unpleasant reminders of dreary sessions with insurance agents and infuriating lectures from parents on the dangers of having a good time. People who think about risk management at all are likely to think of it as a grim necessity, at best.

From another perspective, however, risk management is absolutely riveting, for it is a way to gain more power over events that can change your life. Risk management can help you to seize opportunity, not just to avoid danger. Since good risk management can mean the difference between wealth and poverty, success and failure, life and death, it is worth some of your attention.

Risk management is now emerging as a profession in its own right. People who might have become lawyers, doctors, or engineers are now becoming risk managers, and the best of them are being handsomely rewarded for doing so. Risk managers are starting to make regular appearances at board meetings of major corporations and financial institutions. There are professional risk management journals and there are risk management conventions in Florida. The existence of risk management professionals is, on balance, a good thing, but you should not think that the arrival of the experts lets you off the hook. The experts can help you, but you cannot escape the responsibility of being the chief risk manager of your own life. Only you know what you really want and what you actually believe. You will be the one to suffer most from bad decisions made on your behalf.

The advent of risk management as a distinct profession has created a babble of obscure jargon that can confuse and frustrate the uninitiated. As usual, the experts want to discourage their paying customers from doing too much for themselves. One of the ways they do this is to give unfamiliar names to commonsense ideas, like a doctor telling you that you have a perorbital hematoma when all you have is a black eye.

Fortunately, the basic ideas of risk management are really very simple:

> Risk means being exposed to the possibility of a bad outcome.

> Risk management means taking deliberate action to shift the odds in your favor—increasing the odds of good outcomes and reducing the odds of bad outcomes.

The art of risk management is to adapt and apply these ideas to the particular situations you face in real life—whether you are making decisions in your profession or in your personal life.

The point is not to *become* a risk manager but to become a *better* risk manager, since we are all risk managers already. We make risk decisions every day, often without thinking about it. If you got out of bed this morning, you made a risk decision. If you lit up a cigarette, you made another. If you drove your car to work, you made another. If you put some money in the stock market, you made another. If you took a plane to Philadelphia, you made another (or perhaps two).

I am not suggesting that you agonize over every little choice you make, but I am suggesting that you can and should think more carefully about those decisions that could have important consequences for you. Without realizing it, you might be taking unnecessary or excessive risks. You might be too timid about taking reasonable risks that offer big rewards. You might not be aware of some of the choices available to you that risk management makes possible.

The possible applications of risk management are endless. The financial world is now a hotbed of risk management activity because financial institutions have been particularly vulnerable to surprising disasters, many of which could have been prevented by better risk management. Financial risks have also been easier to quantify than some other kinds of risks. The better-managed financial institutions can now estimate their risk exposure to changes in the financial markets *every day*.

Beyond finance, risk management in one form or another is being applied in medicine, engineering, meteorology, seismology, and many other fields where the consequences of uncertain events can be extreme. The Food and Drug Administration weighs the frequency and severity of a drug's side effects against the drug's effectiveness in fighting disease. Insurance companies price their coverage by estimating the odds and possible damage of a category five hurricane hitting Miami and of a Richter 8 earthquake hitting Los Angeles.

These kinds of calculations are becoming more relevant and more useful as the field of risk management advances, but risk management is not, and will never be, a magic formula that will always give you the right answer. It is a way of thinking that will give you better answers to better questions and by doing so helps you to shift the odds in your favor as you play the game of life.

THE FUTURE IS UNCERTAIN, BUT NOT UNIMAGINABLE

The purpose of risk management is to *improve the future, not to explain the past.* This will seem obvious to everyone but risk management experts, who can become obsessed with fitting historical data to analytically convenient theoretical models, ignoring the possibility that the conditions that caused the historical events to occur will not apply in the future. The main problem with the future, of course, is that no one knows exactly what it will be. Life is uncertain.

People respond in different ways to the prospect of a life full of surprises. Fatalists adopt the attitude that what will be will be—and simply react to events as they unfold. They go with the flow. Fanatics deny uncertainty by believing passionately in their preferred vision of the future, ignoring all other possibilities. They are certain that they know what is going to happen and they act accordingly.

However, others take a more constructive attitude toward uncertainty. Scientists, for example, believe that much of life's uncertainty is due to ignorance, which can be reduced *by finding truth*. A modern geologist is not worried about the unpredictable actions of evil spirits living in rocks, but might be worried about the chances that a nearby volcano will erupt.

Scientists attack ignorance by applying the scientific method. The scientific method depends on logic, observable and repeatable evidence, and the suspension of judgment until that evidence is compelling. Scientists strive for *objectivity,* which is the absence of personal bias in forming theories and interpreting the evidence. A scientist with a personal stake in one theory is prone to overlook or dismiss evidence in favor of a competing theory. Ideally, any scientist should draw the same conclusions from the same facts. Since a personal perspective can subvert the search for truth, *a scientist must be detached.* Detachment not only guards against distortions of the truth; it puts aside any consideration of whether a particular discovery would be useful or valuable. In science, value judgments and personal beliefs are not admissible when weighing the evidence.

Of course, the actual scientific process does not rigidly conform to this ideal, because scientists are all too human. The history of science is as colorful as the rest of human history, a cavalcade of vanity, envy, prejudice, dishonesty, stubbornness, groupthink, and other varieties of human weakness. It is amazing that science has achieved so much, given the vagaries of human nature. Perhaps it is because the scientific method gives too little credit to the creative intuition of real scientists. In any case, scientists do have a distinctive attitude toward uncertainty, characterized by a detached and patient search for verifiable truth.

Unlike the fatalist's passivity, the fanatic's blind faith, and the scientist's detachment, the risk manager has a pragmatic attitude toward uncertainty: *The future may be uncertain but it is not unimaginable and what I do can shift the odds in my favor.*

Unlike the scientist, the risk manager is not trying to be objective; he has an ax to grind, either for himself or someone else. Values and beliefs are to be acted upon, not dismissed. The risk manager's first concern is achieving useful results, not gaining a clearer picture of the truth for its own sake. As we will see, a risk manager has more to gain from some truths than from others, which dampens his enthusiasm for searching for truths that cannot help him decide what to do.

The risk manager, unlike the scientist, does not wait indefinitely for additional evidence to resolve uncertainty. He knows the opportunity to act might not come again so he must act now, even if the right answer is far from obvious.

The risk manager shares the scientist's *intention to be rational,* which sets them both apart from the fatalist and the fanatic. But this shared desire for rationality does not necessarily lead the risk manager and the scientist to the same conclusions from the same set of facts, for their assumptions and motives are often quite different. The scientist uses fact and logic to describe the world more accurately. The risk manager uses fact and logic, to the extent that it is practical, to determine what he *ought to do* to advance his interests.

PINNING DOWN THE MEANING OF RISK

Earlier we said that risk means being exposed to the possibility of a bad outcome. To get any further, we have to decide what we mean by a bad outcome. It is hard to exaggerate the importance of being as clear as possible about the meaning. As the saying goes, "If you don't know where you want to go, any road will get you there."

With the possible exception of death, there is no universal definition of "bad outcome." It depends on the specifics of the situation you are facing. If you are deciding which movie to go to, a bad outcome might be boredom. If you are deciding whether to take your raincoat, a bad outcome might be hypothermia. If you are deciding whether to take out a second mortgage to buy oil futures contracts, a bad outcome might be bankruptcy. To make matters worse, there may be more than one kind of "bad outcome" in a particular situation. You might have to weigh the pain of hypothermia against the pain of looking unfashionable in last year's raincoat.

One way of thinking about this need to be specific about risk is to imagine that your decision is the next move in a game. Before you decide how to move, you have to know what game you are playing and how the score is kept. The consequences of muddled objectives can be devastating.

If you are not the chief executive officer (CEO) of a major corporation, imagine that you are. You are trying to decide whether to build an expensive new factory based on untested but very promising technology. To help you think about the risks involved, I ask you to define the "bad outcome" you want to avoid in making this decision.

You say, "Losing money, obviously."

I ask, "The company's money or your bonus?"

You say, "The company's money."

I let that pass without comment. Now I ask, "By losing the company's money, do you mean taking a hit in this year's reported earnings or in the stock price?"

Being a finance major in business school, you say, "The stock price."

I let that pass also. Now I ask, "The stock price this year or three years from now, after the factory is operating."

Since you are a finance major you know about present value and say, "This year's stock price says it all."

"Maybe," I say, "but what if the stock market doesn't understand the true potential of your new technology and unfairly discounts your stock for three years until the factory is actually finished and working?"

You tire of my annoying questions and have the security guards usher me out of your impressive new headquarters building.

I claim that none of the answers you gave me as CEO were obvious (although some were more politically correct than others). These different meanings of a bad outcome could have led to very different decisions and very different results.

Some questions almost always come up when you are deciding what risk means in your particular situation:

- *How do you measure results?* Is the score tallied in money, mountains climbed, or number of lives saved?
- *What is your starting point for measuring results?* If making money is your game, are you driven by a need to make enough money to retire at 55 and maintain your present standard of living or to make more money than your insufferable brother-in-law Harvey makes?
- *When does the game end?* Are you more concerned about immediate results or longer term results? If you are making choices that you hope will improve your five-year-old child's chances of getting into Harvard, the game ends in thirteen years. If you are about to bet the ranch on 23 red, the game might end in 15 seconds.

There are other questions that will come up when you are trying to be specific about the meaning of risk that applies to your particular situation, but we will leave these for later. Here we just want to emphasize that the clearer your understanding of what you are trying to avoid or to accomplish, the better your chances of making a good risk decision.

AN IDEALIST'S APPROACH
TO MANAGING RISKS

The Holy Grail of risk management is to find the best possible decision to make when faced with uncertainty. Usually we are thrilled to find a decision that is merely good, but there is actually an elegantly logical way to find the very best decision among all conceivable decisions. If this sounds too good to be true, it usually is. I have not forgotten my earlier statement that there are no magic formulas in risk management. But it is worth ignoring the messiness of real life for a moment to look at an idealized decision-making process. Knowing the ideal approach will help us to see what we are really doing when we make a risk decision and to judge the strengths and weaknesses of the more practical methods we use to muddle through in our actual decisions.

Suppose that I offered you the following opportunity: I will draw one card from a standard deck of playing cards. If the card is a spade, I will pay you $100. If it is the ace of spades, I will pay you $1,000. If the card is not a spade, I will pay you nothing. You must decide how much you are willing to pay me to play this game. The right answer to this problem is not apparent, despite the simplicity of the game itself. You might even doubt the existence of one and only one right answer. However, in our ideal world, there really is only one right answer and it is the very best decision you can make under the circumstances, although the answer only works for you, not your brother-in-law Harvey. His beliefs and preferences are different than yours. Let Harvey solve his own problems.

Although we do not know the right answer yet, we can eliminate some possibilities without too much difficulty. Unless you are masochistic, you won't pay me more than $1,000 to play this game, because that would leave you with no possibility whatever of coming out ahead. Although you can pay me nothing and refuse to play, you should be willing to pay me at least some small amount because the game gives you a good chance to win $100 and a shot at winning $1,000, and the worst outcome is that you lose the price of your ticket. I am sure you would pay at least a dime to play. What about a dollar? What about $50? The only question is where you stop and walk away, but you should play at some price. Is the right decision $2, or $10, or $80? At this point our idealized decision-making method comes into play. The game is pictured in Figure 1.1, assuming $20 is the price you are considering paying for a ticket to play.

The diagram shown as Figure 1.1 is an example of a *decision tree*, which is the foundation of risk management. In theory, any risk problem can be represented by a decision tree, although some decision trees are far too large and complex for even the fastest computer to handle.

The decision tree for our card game contains one *uncertain event* (draw a card). There are three possible *outcomes* for the event: ace of spades, spade but not the ace of spades, and not a spade. Each outcome has a *payoff*: $980, $80, or –$20. There is one decision to make: Play or do not play.

Figure 1.1
Card Game

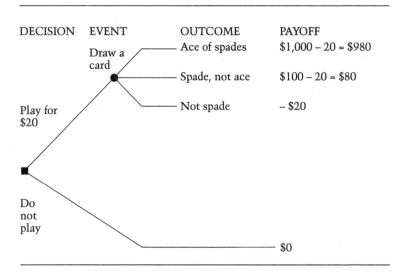

DECISION	EVENT	OUTCOME	PAYOFF
	Draw a card	Ace of spades	$1,000 – 20 = $980
		Spade, not ace	$100 – 20 = $80
Play for $20		Not spade	– $20
Do not play			$0

But we are not finished setting up the problem. We need important information from you to complete the decision tree.

First, we need your *beliefs* about the *probability* of each possible outcome—the odds that you would assign to drawing the ace of spades, the odds of drawing a spade but not the ace, and the odds of not drawing a spade.

We can use common sense to figure the odds. There are 52 cards in the deck and each card has the same chance to be drawn as any other card. So there is one chance in 52 of drawing any particular card such as the ace of spades. Therefore the probability of drawing the ace of spades is $\frac{1}{52}$ or 1.9 percent. There are 13 spades in the deck including the ace, so there are 12 chances in 52 of drawing a spade that is not the ace, giving us a probability of $\frac{12}{52}$ or 23.1 percent. There are 39 cards that are not spades, so there is a 75 percent probability ($\frac{39}{52}$) of drawing one of those. Because there are no other possible outcomes, our probabilities must add up to 100% and they do (1.9 + 23.1 + 75 = 100).

Be aware that your commonsense probability beliefs make the crucial assumptions that I am not a card shark and that the deck is not defective (no missing or duplicate cards). You are making a leap of faith that the game is not rigged against you. For example, a defective deck might be missing the ace of spades, giving you no chance at all of winning the $1,000 prize. This element of faith is always present, to some degree, in any decision you make under uncertainty, for it is you and you alone who must decide and there is never any outside source or expert that you can trust to be completely reliable. In the end, your beliefs are the only beliefs that matter. That is why we called your probability assessments *beliefs*—to remind us of their personal and subjective nature. To keep things simple, we will accept your assumption of a fair game.

As an aside, a rigorous scientist might take a very dim view of what you just did. After all, no one has produced any observations from well-controlled experiments with this particular dealer or deck of cards. He would not accept your assumption of a fair game without evidence. Having no data, the scientist would refuse to assign any odds, would refuse to play, and would pass up any chance of winning the $1,000 prize.

Finally, we need your *preferences* for the payoffs from each outcome. How much pleasure would you get from winning $980 or $80 and how much pain would you feel if you won nothing and lost your entry fee of $20? Vague descriptions of your mood state are not good enough, you must *put numbers* on your preferences. Is winning $980 twice as satisfying as winning $490? Probably not, but is it 1.8 times as satisfying or 1.6 times as satisfying? Every time you make a risk decision you are implicitly assigning numbers to your preferences. I am asking you to make your preferences conscious and explicit.

But how can this be done? It is easy for us to say that we like apples better than oranges. But saying *how much* better seems much harder and possibly irrelevant. It may be hard but it is not irrelevant, because whenever we choose to do something that involves giving up some of one thing to get more of another, we are implicitly saying *by how much* we prefer one to the other. One of the principal assertions of risk management is that it is better to be *explicit* about your preferences, because doing so allows you to apply the power of logic to make a better decision than you would make with fuzzy, dimly perceived preferences. Admittedly, having explicit preferences when choosing fruit at the grocery store may not improve your life very much, but having explicit preferences when plotting a financial strategy for your retirement may improve your life immensely.

Since your choices implicitly embody your preferences, one way to explicitly reveal your preferences is to ask you what you would choose to do in simple situations and deduce your preferences from your answers. This procedure will allow us to apply your newly explicit preferences to more complex decisions.

To explicitly reveal your preferences for money, I start by asking you the following question:

You own a lottery ticket that gives you a 50 percent chance of winning $5,000 and a 50 percent chance of winning nothing. At what price would you sell your ticket?

You think carefully and say "I wouldn't sell my lottery ticket for less than $1,500."

I then ask you the same kind of question again and again, using different amounts of money each time. I take your answers to these questions and do some arithmetic to deduce your explicit preference, or *utility*, for money, which is plotted in Figure 1.2.

Note: When reading utility curves such as this, do not pay attention to the *scale* of the numbers, just the *shape* of the curve that the numbers describe. A utility of 6908 corresponding to a wealth of $0 could just as well have been a utility of 0, and a utility of 7601 corresponding to a wealth of $1,000 could just as well have been a utility of 1. What is significant is that *all the other numbers between 0 and 1 retain their relative relationship and thus preserve*

Figure 1.2
Utility of Money

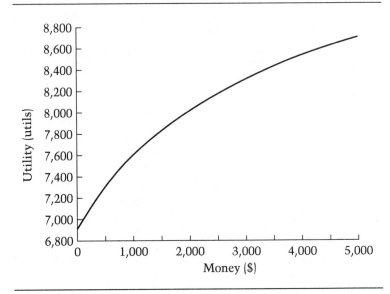

the shape of the utility curve. It is not the absolute of amount of utility that matters but only the relative utilities of different amounts of money as compared to each other.

You can see from Figure 1.2 that your utility curve flattens as the payoff increases. Going from $500 to $1,000 is not as satisfying as going from zero to $500. The next dollar adds less satisfaction than the previous dollar. The tenth cookie is less satisfying than the first cookie. The diminishing satisfaction of getting more and more is a very common characteristic of people's preferences and when this is the case, people are willing to give something up to reduce their risk (their exposure to the possibility of a bad outcome). The experts call this attitude *risk aversion.*

Just as with your beliefs, your preferences are the only preferences that matter for this decision. *You* are the decision maker, so your actions should be logically consistent with *your* preferences and *your* beliefs.

Now we have nearly everything we need to complete our decision tree and to find the one best decision for *you.* Adding your beliefs and preferences, the tree now looks like Figure 1.3, assuming for the moment that you are considering paying $20 to play the game.

Figure 1.3
Decision Tree for the Card Game

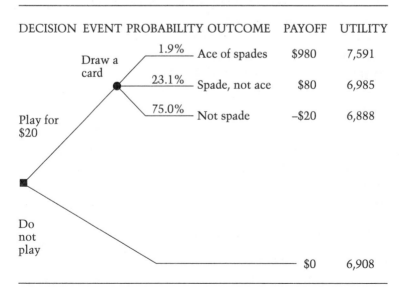

DECISION	EVENT	PROBABILITY	OUTCOME	PAYOFF	UTILITY
	Draw a card	1.9%	Ace of spades	$980	7,591
		23.1%	Spade, not ace	$80	6,985
Play for $20		75.0%	Not spade	–$20	6,888
Do not play				$0	6,908

If you pay $20 to play and the ace of spades is drawn, you gain $980 and experience a satisfaction of 7,591 utils (reading off your utility curve in Figure 1.3), on which $980 corresponds to 7,591 utils). If a spade not the ace is drawn, you gain $80 and experience a satisfaction of 6,985 utils. If no spade is drawn, you lose $20 and experience a satisfaction of 6,888 utils. If you refuse to play, you gain or lose nothing and you experience a satisfaction of 6,908 utils.

Knowing all this might be interesting, but you still do not know what to do. How do you weigh the merits of playing at $20 against the merits of not playing? Playing at $20 involves risk (the possibility of a bad outcome) but also offers the possibility of a reward. Not playing avoids the risk but passes up any chance for the reward. Since you do not know in advance which outcome will occur, how do you decide? How do you weigh the risky choice against the riskless choice? We will use one of the greatest insights in the development of modern risk management.

John Savage, a pioneer in decision theory, showed that it is logically consistent to compare the *expected utility* of a risky choice to the *utility* of a riskless choice. If the expected utility of the risky choice is higher than the utility of the riskless choice, then taking the risk is the logical thing to do. We can weigh two or more risky choices against one another by comparing their expected utilities. The best choice is the choice that has the highest expected utility.

But what, you ask, is expected utility? We will get to that shortly, but first we need to set the stage by clarifying what we mean by logical consistency.

In the end, we want to find a decision that is logically consistent with your beliefs (about the probabilities of all the possible outcomes) and your preferences (the amount of satisfaction you would experience from each possible outcome). You are the decision maker and we want to respect and reflect your interests. We also want to reject any decision that is blatantly illogical when compared to other decisions you would make in similar situations—like the simple gambles we used to assess your utility curve. You do not want to be illogical if you can avoid it. There are several requirements for consistency. As one example, if you prefer A over B, and you prefer B over C, logical consistency requires that you prefer A over C. If you are indifferent between A and B and you are indifferent between B and C, you must be indifferent between A and C. If you pick A over B and you are indifferent between B and C, you must pick A over C. These choices are nothing more than common sense, but consistency can be surprisingly hard to achieve when making decisions that involve risk.

Fortunately, using Savage's insight on expected utility, we can avoid these and other logical blunders. We are going to calculate the *expected utility* of each alternative decision and select the decision that has the highest expected utility. Then we are done. We will have chosen the best possible decision that is consistent with your beliefs, your preferences, and the facts of this particular situation.

Now, finally, what is expected utility? Expected utility is a weighted average of the utilities of all the possible outcomes that could flow from a particular decision, where higher-probability outcomes count more than lower-probability outcomes in calculating the average. For example, if a particular decision gives you an 80 percent chance of experiencing 1,000 utils and a 20 percent chance of experiencing –200 utils, the expected utility of making this decision is:

.80 × 1000 plus .20 × (–200) equals 760 expected utils

This calculation is intuitively reasonable because everything else being equal, an outcome with an 80 percent probability is much more important to your likely satisfaction than an outcome with 20 percent probability. The decision with the highest expected utility is anticipated to produce higher satisfaction, averaged over all its possible outcomes, than any other decision. In other words, each alternative decision puts you on a different path into the future and the *best* decision puts you on a path that offers the highest satisfaction on average, considering the likelihood of all its possible outcomes along the way.

Using expected utility to identify the best decision makes intuitive sense, but some fancy mathematics is required to demonstrate that maximizing expected utility is indeed the right thing to do (and there is lively debate among the experts on the finer points of this principle).

Finally, we have all that we need to determine the best decision for you. We have identified the decision you must make (whether to buy a $20 ticket to play this game). We have identified the uncertain event (drawing the card), all its possible outcomes (ace of spades, spade not the ace, not a spade), and the payoff from each outcome ($980, $80, or –$20). We have assessed your beliefs about the probabilities of each outcome and your preferences for the payoff from each outcome (expressed in units of utility). Last but not least, we have determined your objective (to find the decision that offers you the highest expected utility).

We now calculate the expected utility of each decision you could make. If you pay $20 to play, you have a 1.9 percent probability of 7,591 utils, a 23.1 percent probability of 6,985 utils and 75 percent probability of 6,888 utils. Your expected utility of playing is:

$$(.019 \times 7,591) + (.231 \times 6,985) + (.75 \times 6,888) = 6,924$$

If you do not play, you have a 100 percent probability of 6,908 utils. Your expected utility of not playing is:

$$1.0 \times 6,908 = 6,908$$

Because paying $20 to play has a higher expected utility (6,924 utils) than not playing (6,908 utils), you should be willing to pay at least $20 to play. In fact, you should be willing to pay more than $20.

To find the very highest price that you should be willing to pay, we find the price that offers the same expected utility as not playing, namely 6,908 utils. At that price you are indifferent between playing and not playing.

By calculating the expected utilities of a range of ticket prices we see from the following list that a price of $35 offers the same expected utility (6,908) as not playing:

Ticket Price	Expected Utility
$20	6,924
$25	6,918
$30	6,913
$35	6,908
$40	6,903

Now you know exactly what to do. If I charge you less than $35, you should play. However, if I try to charge any more than $35, you should refuse to play.

This is the *best possible decision* for you to make if you are to be logically consistent with your stated preferences and beliefs. It is what you *ought to do* if faced with this situation. Remember that we are not trying to be scientific and search for truth, we are trying to make you better off. An academic psychologist might define the problem very differently, trying to predict what people, in general, *will actually do* if faced with this type of situation. Some people might be illogical and refuse to play. Others might pay too much to play. The psychologist is not giving advice, but is a neutral observer trying to discover patterns in human behavior. It is not his job to tell you what you ought to do in this particular situation. He is being descriptive and we are being prescriptive. He is detached, but we have an agenda.

Knowing the decision that you *ought* to make, what do you do if that decision seems wrong? If you feel uncomfortable with the decision dictated by logic, you may want to reconsider your assessments of your probability beliefs and preferences. Sometimes another iteration produces a more accurate picture of what your beliefs and preferences really are. But be careful that you do not bias your analysis by artificially forcing it to converge to a predetermined result that has an irrational appeal to you. The best decision is not always the one that you are instinctively drawn to.

Earlier we discussed the importance of precisely defining what we mean by risk. In this example, we did just that. First, we decided to keep score by quantifying the satisfaction you would derive from gaining or losing money (what we called your utility curve). Second, we did not include any other ways of keeping score, such as the forgone pleasure of my company if you refused to play the game. Third, we decided that the game ended with the drawn card and we completely ignored anything that might happen after the game, such as losing your winnings at next week's poker game.

The risk in this example is very specific. By buying a ticket, you take a risk by exposing yourself to a 75 percent chance of a bad outcome (losing the price of your ticket). You are willing to take this risk (up to a ticket price of $35) because you feel this risk is outweighed by the 1.9 percent chance at winning the $1,000 prize and the 23.1 percent chance at winning the $100 prize.

We went through this example to illustrate an idealized method for managing risks, even though many real-life risk problems are too complex to solve in this crisp and precise fashion. Again, in real life there are no magic formulas. However, our idealized risk management method captures virtually every feature of real risk problems and it tells us *how we ought to solve risk problems* (if only we could). It fully reflects our risk management philosophy of acting on *your* beliefs and *your* preferences to improve *your* future by helping *you* make better risk decisions. We are not conducting a scientific experiment to find new truth that describes the world more accurately. We are not detached or objective.

Our card game is a simple decision tree. To tackle harder problems, we add more decisions, more events, more outcomes, and more complex beliefs and preferences. If we can properly identify how all these additional elements relate to each other, we can construct a decision tree that can, in principle, be solved to reveal the very best decision—if only we have fast enough computers or large enough brains to do so. A large decision tree can be solved by successively transforming its bushy branches into simple branches that contain simple gambles.

Newcomers to decision trees often have difficulty with the concept of utility. The term "utilitarian" comes to mind and it has acquired an unpleasant connotation. A utilitarian is thought to be the sort of person who would cheerfully grind up his grandmother for soup if the grandmother's pain would be less than the diners' collective pleasure. Rest assured that we do not make such proposals here. Apart from logical consistency, we have little to say about what your preferences ought to be. You are perfectly free to value your grandmother above all else in the world, if you want to. We merely suggest that you do, in fact, have preferences. They influence your behavior every day whether you acknowledge it or not. You choose to do one thing over another partly because you prefer one thing to another, to a certain *degree*. We claim that you will usually be better off if you can express your preferences clearly and act on them rationally. We are *not* suggesting that this process is always easy or painless.

At a more technical level, one difficulty with decision trees is that they can become very large very quickly, growing exponentially as more decisions, events, and outcomes are added. A tree with 10 alternative decisions, 10 events for each decision, and 10 possible outcomes for each event has 1,000 possible outcomes to evaluate ($10 \times 10 \times 10$). Change 10 to 20 and you have 8,000 outcomes to grapple with, and so on.

Consequently, most real-life risk problems of any importance have to be simplified to be solved. The best risk managers are those that can simplify without sacrificing the essentials. Much of this book is about the progress we are making in doing just that.

By using our idealized risk management method as a benchmark, we have a much better grip on the essentials and what we might be sacrificing by taking shortcuts or making simplifying approximations. Judging ourselves against the ideal forces us to think more clearly about our problem: to sift the wheat from the chaff; to break the problem into smaller, more manageable pieces; to avoid unnecessary errors in logic; and to use the results more intelligently.

Chapter 2

BELIEFS AND PREFERENCES

Our simple example of the card game introduced all the important elements of any risk management problem. We constructed a *decision tree* that linked every *alternative decision* with the *uncertain events* that could flow from that decision. We identified all the possible *outcomes* of each uncertain event and to each outcome we assigned a *probability*, a *payoff*, and the *utility* of that payoff. Since you were the decision maker, we used *your beliefs* to assign probabilities to each outcome and *your preferences* to assign utilities to each payoff. To be logically consistent with your beliefs and preferences, we found the best possible decision by finding the decision that offered you the *highest expected utility*.

So in our ideal world, we manage risk by applying a particular logic to your beliefs and preferences to find the best decision for you to make. Clearly, beliefs and preferences are at the heart of risk management. Some risk managers get into deep trouble by losing track of the beliefs and preferences implicitly imbedded in what they do. For example, in 1994, many financial institutions lost very large amounts of money when interest rates rose sharply and unexpectedly. Their losses were partly attributable to a belief, apparently based on recent history and not reexamined as conditions changed, that interest rates could never move that far that fast.

ASSESSING YOUR BELIEFS

We keep saying that you, as decision maker, must act on your beliefs. But what if you don't have a clue about the probabilities of the possible outcomes? It doesn't matter—you cannot get off the hook. You have to make a decision, because even if you do nothing you are doing something. Doing nothing has consequences just as any other decision has consequences. Doing nothing can mean missing valuable opportunities or allowing threats to materialize. Doing nothing can also mean keeping your options open and gaining new information. You will decide, no matter what, and whatever decision you make, you are implicitly acting on your probability beliefs, even if you don't know what they are. It is better to know what they are.

For example, if you drove your car to work today, I claim that you believed, implicitly, that there was less than a 10 percent probability of being in a fatal car accident. Dying is usually considered to be a very bad outcome, and if at all probable, would easily overwhelm the prospect of a good day at the office. Unless you had suicidal preferences, a 10 percent or higher chance of death would keep you at home. Therefore, you assigned less than a 10 percent probability to dying in a car accident today.

Doing a better job of judging the odds helps you make better risk decisions. But how do you acquire informed and reasonable probability beliefs if you are not a statistician and do not intend to become one? For some kinds of decisions, common sense is good enough, either because the difference between being right or wrong is not too great or because your guess is going to be as good as anyone else's (even a statistician's).

In our card game, where drawing a card was the uncertain event, you didn't really need my help to assign the odds to the three possible outcomes. It was just common sense, as long as you believed that I was not a card shark and the deck was not defective. Hiring a statistician would not have helped you. You also would not need any help to assign a 50 percent probability to a coin flip turning out heads or to assign a one-in-six chance of rolling a three with a single die. In both cases, all of the possible outcomes are easily identified and all of the outcomes are equally likely, so figuring the odds is simple and reasonable people would agree on what those odds were.

Assessing probabilities is more complicated when the probability of one outcome is affected by whether another outcome has occurred. For example, the probability of drawing a spade from a deck of cards on the second try depends on what card was drawn on the first try (assuming that the first card was not put back in the deck). If the first card was not a spade, then there are 13 spades remaining in a deck with 51 cards remaining, giving a probability of $^{13}/_{51}$. If the first card *was* a spade, then there are 12 spades remaining in a deck with 51 cards remaining, giving a probability of $^{12}/_{51}$. This interdependency among the probabilities of different outcomes is a very common feature of risk problems. If not taken into account, it may lead to a decision that is seriously off the mark.

So far we have assumed that all the possible outcomes are clearly identifiable and that their relative probabilities can be calculated by applying the right logic. There is no reason to doubt or to argue about the outcomes or their probabilities. There is still risk involved, of course, because the outcomes are uncertain, but there is no uncertainty about the odds themselves.

Playing roulette in a fairly run Las Vegas casino is a perfect example of this type of uncertainty. All of the possible outcomes are clearly defined (23 red, for example) and the odds of each outcome can be determined by simple arithmetic. Everyone who does the arithmetic correctly will agree on the odds.

But what if the uncertainties that you face are not so tidy? What if you are not sure about what all the outcomes could be or how they might be related to one another? What if there is no obviously correct way to assign probabilities to the outcomes?

Meteorologists find themselves in this position every day. Even though there are vast amounts of current and historical weather data available, no one has been able to construct the equivalent of a roulette wheel for weather. There is no single set of possible weather outcomes and probabilities that all the experts agree to, because the number of possible outcomes is enormous and the mechanism producing the outcomes is too complex and too poorly understood. The very definition of a weather outcome is difficult to pin down. What is a sunny day? No clouds at all from sunrise to sunset? Mostly sunny most of the time? No more than 10 percent cloud cover for at least 80 percent of the time from sunrise to sunset? There is no single right answer. If you want a nice day for a picnic, your definition of a sunny day will be different than that of a farmer whose annual income depends on the cumulative amount of sunlight reaching the ground during the growing season.

Some people draw a sharp distinction between the two types of uncertainty that we have just described. They refer to the roulette wheel type of uncertainty by the term *risk* and reserve the term *uncertainty* for the weather type of uncertainty. There is nothing wrong with these descriptions of two situations that definitely seem different. The risky situation is crisply defined and the uncertain situation is not. But for the risk manager it is a distinction without a difference and it should not affect the ultimate decision that is made. How can this be?

Suppose you were offered the choice to play one of two different games. The first game offers a $1,000 prize if a coin toss comes up heads. The second game offers a $1,000 prize if a white marble is drawn from an opaque urn containing 100 marbles, an *unknown* number of which are white and the remainder black. The marbles were placed in the urn by a blindfolded and secluded Price Waterhouse auditor who has no stake in the outcome of the game and who is unaware that the game is being played. No one has seen the contents of the urn, or the auditor, since.

The coin game has sharply defined outcomes and probabilities—there is definitely a 50 percent probability of winning. Because the odds are known, some would say that this game involves risk, but does not involve uncertainty.

The urn game is a different matter. You don't know how many white marbles are actually in the urn in front of you. If the urn contains 20 white marbles and 80 black marbles, there is a 20 percent probability of winning. If the urn contains 60 white marbles and 40 black marbles, there is a 60 percent probability of winning, and so on. If you don't know anything about the contents of the urn, how can you assess the probability of winning? Because the odds themselves are not definitely known, some would say this game involves uncertainty rather than risk. You know more about the coin game, so it would be natural to prefer the coin game to the urn game—to choose a game of risk over a game of uncertainty, everything else being equal.

But think about the urn game again. Did I give you any reason at all to suspect that the urn sitting in front of you has more black marbles than white marbles? More white marbles than black marbles? No, I did not. All possibilities for the contents of the urn should seem equally likely to you. If so, you have no reason to believe that drawing a white marble from the urn is any more or less likely than drawing a black marble from the urn—from your perspective, there is a 50 percent chance of white and a 50 percent chance of black. In other words, you should assign the same probability to winning the urn game as you assign to winning the coin game.

And to take it one step further, it can be shown that there is no rational basis (in our idealized world) for choosing the coin game over the urn game or vice versa. For decision-making purposes, they are identical games.

Therefore it is not relevant to you, the decision maker, that you know the true odds of winning the coin game but do not know the true odds of winning the urn game. Suppose that an omniscient observer knows the truth—that the urn sitting in front of you actually contains 90 white marbles and 10 black marbles and therefore that the true odds of winning are 90 percent. If you don't know that and cannot find out, you obviously cannot act on it. At the point of decision, you have to act on what you believe and in this example you have no reason to believe that the chance of winning the urn game is anything but 50 percent.

By the way, from the scientist's perspective, the urn game represents a state of pure ignorance. There is no experimental data available from this game that sheds any light whatever on the actual number of black or white marbles in the urn in front of you. There are no experiments done in similar situations that would yield any relevant evidence. There is no theory that can determine how many white marbles should be in the urn. Therefore, the scientist would say that the true proportion of white marbles to black marbles is unknown and so the probability of drawing a white marble cannot be assessed. She will have nothing more to say, unless and until some drawings from the urn have been observed.

Clearly, the scientist is of no help to you in deciding whether to play the urn game, but that is not her job. Her job is to describe the process of the game more accurately, to search for the truth, which in this case is the actual proportion of black to white marbles in the urn (which our omniscient observer knows to be 90 percent). Whether you decide to play this game is of no concern to her, even if you will never get another chance to play and miss your shot at the $1,000 prize. If you play, she will observe the outcome with detachment and count that as one observation among the many that she hopes to see. Once she has observed many outcomes, she may have something to say about what might be in the urn. If she is curious about the truth, she may ponder the problem long after anyone is playing the game and has anything to win or lose.

Unlike the observing and detached scientist, you as a risk manager must make a decision to play or not play the urn game based on your beliefs, even if you are very uncomfortable with the "truth" of those beliefs. In other situations, of course, you may have opportunities to gain more information before committing to an action, and it may be wise to do so. But acquiring more information usually means delay and expense, and you must still decide, now, whether acquiring that information is worth that delay and expense. The imperative to decide, based on your beliefs at the moment, is always there.

PREFERENCES

Most people don't like risk, in most situations, most of the time. We called this dislike *risk aversion* in Chapter 1. Someone who was risk averse would not play a game that offered an equal chance of winning $50,000 and losing $50,000, because the satisfaction of winning would be much less than the pain of losing. In order to play, that person would demand a larger prize and/or a greater chance of winning the prize. In our card game in Chapter 1, we knew that you were risk averse—expressed by your utility curve that flattened out as the payoff increased. If we had assumed even greater risk aversion (by an even flatter utility curve as the payoff increased), your decision would have been different. Your maximum tolerable price to play the game would have gone down.

It should be clear by now that the right risk decision for you depends on the combined influence of your beliefs about the probabilities of the possible outcomes and your preferences for the payoffs resulting from those outcomes.

We have just discussed the necessarily subjective and personal nature of the beliefs you act upon. It is self-evident that your preferences are inherently subjective and personal as well. This means that risk decisions are inherently personal and subjective, so "experts" pushing one-size-fits-all solutions are to be viewed with caution and skepticism. If a decision has important and uncertain consequences, you should try to find the decision that fits you, not someone else.

Just as you might have difficulty expressing your beliefs as probabilities, you might have difficulty expressing your preferences as a utility curve. However, as we mentioned in Chapter 1, under some circumstances, it can be done. By asking you to choose between simple gambles, an expert could construct your utility curve, which could be used to represent your preferences in more complex situations.

The presence or absence of risk aversion is by far the most important aspect of your preferences and will profoundly influence the kinds of decisions you should make. Indeed, the phenomenon of risk aversion is the driving force behind risk management. Because most decisions are made by people who are risk averse, risk managers can make a good living by helping people to avoid or reduce risks that don't offer sufficient rewards.

Although risk aversion usually prevails, there are some interesting exceptions. Many people are willing to accept very unfair odds if they think there is little to lose and much to gain, even if the gain is highly improbable. Odds are *unfair* if the expected result is a loss. An example of unfair odds would be a coin flip giving a 50–50 chance of either winning $100 or losing $110. The expected result of this game would be a loss of $5 = [.50 × 100 + .50 × (–110)]. If you played this game 1,000 times, your cumulative average loss would almost certainly be close to $5. Most people would not play this game, not once, not 1,000 times, even if their risk aversion were extremely low. It seems obvious that this proposition is not attractive.

But consider another example of unfair odds. In front of me is an urn with 1,000 marbles, one of which is black and 999 of which are white. If I draw a white ball from the urn, you lose $1, but if I draw the single black ball you win $900. The expected result from this game is a loss of about 10 cents [.999 × (–$1) + .001 × $900]. The odds are unfair, but would you be tempted to play this game? After all, the worst that can happen is that you lose $1 and you have a shot at winning $900. If you are willing to play, even though you know the odds are unfair, you are not being risk averse. You are actually being a risk seeker, in this particular situation. A strictly risk-averse person never voluntarily accepts unfair odds.

In July 1998, the roads from New York to Connecticut were clogged with people trying to buy Powerball lottery tickets. The odds of winning were pitifully small and stacked against the ticket buyers (after all, the lottery sponsors were making a lot of money without taking any risk themselves). This was definitely a game with unfair odds. A risk-averse person would never buy a ticket because the expected result is a loss. However, the prize had reached $250 million and a ticket only cost a dollar. For many people, the mere possibility of winning $250 million with a $1 ticket overwhelmed any concern about the odds, however slim and unfair they might have been. Were the buyers of the Powerball tickets irrational? Not people whose preferences were genuinely skewed toward risk taking in that type of situation and who had realistic beliefs about the odds of winning. They made a reasonable risk decision that reflected their beliefs and preferences. Those who had grossly exaggerated beliefs about the odds of winning or those who spent their life savings on lottery tickets are harder to rationalize.

Many, if not most, of the risk lovers who bought lottery tickets would be risk averse in other situations where the potential losses are much greater. As we mentioned in Chapter 1, you don't have just one utility curve. You have many utility curves, and the relevant curve depends on the particular situation you are facing. Your curves may not be smooth. They may have irregular bumps and discontinuities. They may shift over time as your life changes.

Because the task of explicitly assigning numbers to preferences can be difficult and time consuming, it is usually neglected in actual risk management applications. Instead, we make some crude assumptions and move on. The most common assumption is that decision makers are risk averse and that assumption is often good enough to tell us some very useful things about what we should do. Risk-averse people do not voluntarily accept unfair odds. Risk-averse people usually give up some upside to avoid some downside. Risk-averse people are willing to pay something for good risk management advice.

Chapter 3

COMBINING ART AND SCIENCE

Volatility and Correlation

In our ideal world of risk management, everything is very logical and systematic. We structure our problem as a decision tree, linking all the uncertain events, all the possible outcomes, the payoff for each of the outcomes, and all the alternative decisions that we could make. We put numbers on our probability beliefs and our preferences. We have the clear objective of maximizing our expected utility. We do the math and we find the best possible decision. End of story.

If only life were so simple. In real situations, there may be so many uncertain events, possible outcomes, and decisions to consider that the problem is far too big to solve in our idealized way. We may not even be able to identify all the events, outcomes, and decisions, making our decision tree incomplete and potentially misleading. We might have to try to predict the actions of others, knowing that they are trying to predict our actions, creating a tangle of endless possibilities. Our preferences and beliefs might be hard to pin down. Even if we think that we could describe the problem accurately and solve it, we may not have the time or money to do so. We need a way to bridge the gap between the ideal and the real, because we have to make decisions and take the consequences of those decisions.

Diehard traditionalists might dismiss the effort to be more logical and systematic about making risk decisions. Because any idealized model will inevitably fall short of reality anyway, why not just make decisions the old-fashioned way—with intuition and gut feel, drawing from experience? There is no evidence that Admiral Nelson, J. P. Morgan, or Harry

Truman used decision trees. They used inspiration and seasoned judgment. The more we learn about how the brain works, the more we understand that a shockingly large fraction of its activity takes place beyond our awareness and control. The unconscious mind works on problems in the back room and announces the results to the conscious mind in the form of inspiration and judgment. Viewed from this perspective, our decision trees look like clever little Tinkertoys that might be amusing to play with but that are useless for real work.

Taking the opposite view, diehard idealists might dismiss intuitive decision making as uninformed, sloppy, irrational, myopic, and wedded to the past. Seat-of-the-pants decision makers are dangerous relics who are good only for fighting the last war. Failing to think clearly and logically about all the available facts is the definition of stupidity and is a terrible waste of the cognitive power of the brain. It makes no sense to make unnecessary errors and omissions.

The commonsense view is that good decision making usually comes from a combination of art and science, of sound judgment and logical analysis. When the launch director pushed the button to send *Apollo 11* to the Moon, he did not say, "It feels good, let's do it." He got as much information as he could about the status of the *Saturn 5* rocket and thought very hard about the many disaster scenarios that the team had visualized and analyzed for years. He was also keenly aware of the urgency to act, because delay could mean that the Soviet Union would reach the Moon first. Only after using his judgment to weigh the risks and rewards, some of which were logically analyzed and some of which were not, did he push the button. It is very hard to believe that all the logical analysis and fact-finding that preceded the launch was wasted just because, in the end, he made a judgment call. It is also very hard to believe that a robot or computer would have made a better launch director than would a human being with good judgment.

Or consider the work of a brain surgeon. Medical science has come a long way since primitive healers drilled holes in their patients' heads to cure headaches. Medical scientists know the anatomy of the brain in much greater detail. They know most of the basic functions of different regions of the brain, allowing them to assess the probable consequences of different types of brain damage or disease. They have developed sensitive tools, such as magnetic resonance imaging, to detect and locate many types of brain abnormalities. They have developed surgical instruments that are much more precise than the crude drills of the primitive healers. Last but not least, they have developed anesthetics that are much better than homebrew wine.

Despite this impressive scientific progress, we still regard brain surgery as a risky proposition, and for good reason. The brain is still deeply mysterious, so the effects of cutting into it can be surprising. A slight slip of the knife can kill or permanently disable the patient. Ironically, as medical science advances, there is an understandable temptation to propose riskier procedures in the hope of curing formerly intractable conditions. This drive for better surgical techniques is how progress occurs, but if you are the patient it may occur at the cost of your life. So when the time comes to open up your skull, you don't call a medical scientist, you call the best brain surgeon you can find. Someone who not only has up-to-date knowledge and tools but who also has demonstrated a superb touch with the knife and the ability to make sound judgments under conditions of great uncertainty and pressure.

A good risk manager is like the launch director and the brain surgeon, using facts and logic as far as they will take him and making a judgmental leap to arrive at a final decision. The main contribution of risk analysis is to make those judgmental leaps a bit shorter and less dangerous than they would otherwise be. Because risk management requires both risk analysis and risk judgment, it is a combination of art and science. Today, if you don't have any analytical models, you are unlikely to be a good risk manager. If all you have are analytical models, you cannot be a risk manager at all.

VOLATILITY

In our idealized world of risk management, we did not place any restrictions at all on the nature of the uncertainty that you could analyze. It could be anything—financial, medical, meteorological, political, geological, or metaphysical—as long as you could identify all the possible outcomes, assess their probabilities, and link them together in a decision tree. Every risk problem was unique, self-contained, and solvable. This capability is powerful, but it makes it hard to apply lessons learned in previous situations to new, but similar situations. If we can recognize recurring patterns or tendencies across similar kinds of problems, we can develop some generalizations and rules of thumb that will save us time and improve our ability to make better risk judgments. Volatility is one such generalization that is useful in thinking about many, but not all, types of risk. Loosely speaking, a situation that has a wide range of possible outcomes has higher volatility, and perhaps higher risk, than a situation with a narrow range of possible outcomes. A person with a volatile personality might be riskier to your welfare than someone with a more stable personality. Volatile weather might carry more risk than more stable weather. Volatile stocks might be riskier to hold than more stable stocks.

A simple example of using volatility would be a coin toss game with a 50–50 chance of losing $1,000 or winning $2,000. This game has higher volatility and is surely riskier than an otherwise identical coin toss game with a 50–50 chance of losing $100 or winning $200. We might define each game's volatility as the difference between its two possible outcomes. The high volatility game would have volatility of $3,000 [$2,000 − (−$1,000)] and the low volatility game would have volatility of $300 [$200 − (−$100)]. Our simple measure has relevance to volatility because it approximately captures the large difference in the range of outcomes that each game could produce. Knowing that one 50–50 coin toss game had a volatility of $3,000 and another had a volatility of

$300 could be useful information and perhaps a reasonable way to compare the risks of different games. The more volatile game has a much wider range of possible outcomes, which in this case greatly increases the potential pain of losing. Intuitively, the volatile game is the riskier game (but be aware that this is not necessarily true in other situations).

So the concept of volatility can be useful shorthand to roughly describe the risks of different situations, just as the concept of weight is useful shorthand to roughly describe the size of different people. But even more important, thinking about volatility forces you to ask yourself the fundamental question: "Volatility of what?" What is it that really worries me about this situation and can I express it clearly and specifically? If you can, you have taken a giant step toward quantifying risk, because statistical measures can capture the essence of volatility, and hopefully risk, in a set of numbers.

Quantification of risk is the most powerful aspect of modern risk management because it brings the clarity and logical consistency of mathematics to the analysis of complex uncertainties than are far beyond anyone's unaided powers of intuition or judgment. You can build a kite without mathematics but not a 747. In Chapter 6 we see how the quantification of volatility has revolutionized the management of financial risk.

Whether volatility is a useful concept to represent risk is highly dependent on finding a level of generality that works in your particular situation. If your measure of volatility is too narrow and specific, you may omit important aspects of risk. If your measure of volatility is too broad and general, you may obscure important aspects of risk.

Return to the examples we mentioned previously. In the case of the volatile personality, it seems unlikely that trying to measure "personality volatility" in one number is going to get us very far. What single number could capture the essence of the rich variety of possible behaviors? Would it help you to know that Harry has a personality volatility of 2.6 compared to the norm of 1.0? Without knowing more, you would have no way of judging whether Harry was unusually entertaining or unusually dangerous. It would not help you make the risk decision of going or not going on a camping trip with Harry. From our point of view as risk managers, a single measure of personality volatility would be far too general, obscuring too much vital information. Does Harry's impulsiveness express itself in humor, moodiness, or violence? Something more specific, such as the volatility of Harry's testosterone level could be a useful measure of risk in particular situations. Volatile testosterone might present a real and measurable risk to someone camping in the wilderness with Harry.

Weather volatility is another concept that is too general to be useful as a measure of risk. So many different weather variables have so many different kinds of consequences that any single number would be meaningless. However, something more specific, such as volatility of rainfall or temperature or wind velocity could be a useful measure of risk in particular situations. Volatile rainfall might present a real and measurable risk to a farmer. Volatile temperature might present a real and measurable risk to a mountain climber. Volatile wind velocity could present a real and measurable risk to a fishing boat captain.

Volatility can be a very useful yardstick for risk, but it has two main pitfalls. We have already discussed one of those pitfalls: A poorly chosen volatility measure can obscure or omit important dimensions of risk by measuring the volatility of the wrong thing. If you are faced with the possibility of freezing to death, it is not a good idea to measure risk by looking at the volatility of barometric pressure.

The other main pitfall of volatility is simply that volatility is not always bad and therefore not always a risk, since we associate risk with bad outcomes. Suppose you could choose between two coin toss games. The first game gives a 50–50 chance of losing $1,000 and winning $2,000. The second game gives a 50–50 chance of losing $1,000 or winning $5,000. By our measure of volatility for these games, the second game is far more volatile than the first: $6,000 compared to $3,000. But is the second game riskier? Clearly not, because both games have identical downsides—each presents a 50 percent chance of losing $1,000—they must have the same risk. Our volatility measure led us astray because it did not distinguish between good volatility (a greater range of possible rewards) and bad volatility (a greater range of possible losses). Because the second game has the same risk and a greater potential reward, it is the obvious choice. If we had shown you just the volatility measure without showing you the actual structure underneath it, you might have picked the second game and made the wrong risk decision.

Suppose you have avoided these pitfalls and have selected a definition and measure of volatility that is a good representation of the risk that you face. How do you come up with the actual numbers that allow you to calculate the volatility that you may face under various alternative decisions?

An obvious place to start is to look at history. Suppose that observations of actual outcomes over the past five years are consistent with a volatility of 10 units. Unless you have good reasons to believe otherwise, you might reasonably assume that volatility will be 10 units in the future and make your decision accordingly. Unfortunately, you often have good reasons to believe otherwise. As we all know, history can teach us valuable lessons, but it cannot automatically give us an accurate picture of the future—and it is only the future that we care about when we make risk decisions.

Conditions may have changed so much that past volatility gives us very little information about future volatility. Looking at the volatility of foreign exchange rates in the 1950s tells us virtually nothing about the volatility of foreign exchange rates over the next year. In the 1950s, the major governments of the world were operating under an agreement to maintain fixed exchange rates. That agreement no longer exists, allowing exchange rates to fluctuate widely. Exchange rate volatility during the 1950s is no longer a good indicator of future volatility.

On a far grander scale, some scientists believe that the volatility of Earth's temperature has been much lower during the last 10,000 years than was typical for the preceding million years, creating an unusually favorable environment for the rise of human civilization. For most of its history, Earth has been subject to large fluctuations in average temperature, producing an ice age every few thousand years or so. Extrapolating recent history's relatively stable and temperate climate far into the future could be unjustified. If there is a real possibility that we are overdue for the beginning of the next ice age, we might, for example, want to make different risk decisions about policies to prevent global warming.

In most risky situations, historical volatility lies somewhere between irrelevant and compelling. You are the decision maker so you have to use your judgment in applying the apparent lessons of the past. What factors contributed to past volatility? Are they still in place or are new factors more important? Do you believe that even further change lies ahead? These questions are primarily of informed belief rather than statistics—another example of the important difference between risk analysis and risk management.

If you are not a professional risk expert, all of this discussion may seem too obvious to mention. Everyone knows that the past is, at best, an imperfect guide to the future. However, risk experts, like experts in other fields, are prone to fall in love with their tools and this love can lead to severe myopia. Experts can be tempted to define problems in ways that fit their tools rather than ways that fit the actual situation. Statistics is a favorite tool of the risk expert and the past is much more accessible to statistics than the future. Only the past has the data points that statistics craves. So the unwary risk expert may exaggerate the importance of the historical data that allow him to use his favorite tools and to arrive at a definite solution, even if it is the solution to the wrong problem.

Many models of risk make two dubious assumptions: first, that historical data are sufficient to predict future volatility and second, that future volatility will be constant over time, which is rarely the case in a changing world. Risk analysts may be tempted to make these dubious assumptions because they make the math much simpler and because they relieve the analyst of responsibility for making difficult judgments about the future. There have been many fiascoes in the financial world that were attributable, at least in part, to leaning too hard on statistical models that were overly dependent on historical data and uninformed by seasoned judgment about future possibilities.

For example, following the collapse of Communism in Russia, a market began to develop for Russian securities. As more players entered this market, traders began to feel confident that these markets, though still primitive, would behave more or less like other more established markets (more volatile and less liquid). Statistics from established markets were used as analogies in estimating the volatility and liquidity of the Russian market. The early traders knew that the market was risky but they believed that they would gain a valuable competitive advantage as the market grew over time. But then, in 1998, the Russian government decided that it would rather not honor some of its debt. This event was not supposed to happen. Of course, this was not the first time in history that a government had reneged. Several Latin American countries have done it more than once. Why was this possibility dismissed? In any event, the market collapsed and exploded in volatility and illiquidity—far beyond what was assumed possible by the pioneer traders. Losses were very large and very embarrassing. An optimistic volatility assumption had cost some of the pioneer traders dearly.

Despite these dangers, the concept of volatility as a quantifiable description of risk is often a good starting point for managing many types of risks.

CORRELATION

Whenever volatility is used as a quantifiable measure of risk, correlation is not far behind. Correlation allows us to judge the combined volatility of two or more things that are volatile. If you own two high-volatility stocks, how volatile is the combined value of the two stocks? In many cases, the two stocks combined will be less volatile, per dollar invested, than either stock by itself. Correlation can tell us by how much volatility will be reduced by owning the two-stock portfolio rather than a one-stock portfolio. When combining volatilities, 2 + 2 does not always equal 4. Correlation makes it possible for us to say that 2 + 2 equals 3.2.

Although it has fancy mathematical definitions in particular risk models, the basic idea of correlation is simple. Two things are correlated if they show a tendency to change in tandem with each other.

Rainfall in your neighborhood swamp is correlated with the number of mosquitoes in your backyard. Higher rainfall usually means higher numbers of mosquitoes. Because rainfall and mosquitoes tend to move in the same direction—if rainfall increases, mosquitoes probably increase—they are positively correlated.

Rainfall in Iowa is correlated with the price of corn. Higher rainfall usually means larger corn crops, which usually mean lower corn prices. Because rainfall and corn prices tend to move in opposite directions—if rainfall increases, corn prices probably decrease—they are negatively correlated.

It is important that you do not confuse correlation with cause and effect. Two things may appear to be correlated even though they have nothing whatever to do with each other. In both of our rainfall examples, correlation was a consequence of cause and effect. Rainfall in the swamp caused (or at least contributed to) more mosquitoes. Rainfall in Iowa caused (or at least contributed to) lower corn prices. But suppose that over the last five years, both Iowa and the swamp had unusually rainy conditions, so we observed both lower corn prices and more mosquitoes in your backyard. A statistician would observe a negative correlation between corn prices and mosquitoes over the five-year period. But did lower corn prices cause more mosquitoes? Clearly not. If you see a correlation, you should not automatically assume that one thing causes or contributes to the other. You might not want to make a decision based on the supposition that corn prices and mosquitoes will be negatively correlated in the future.

But what if the swamp were in Iowa? Although lower corn prices still do not cause more mosquitoes, they are both affected by the same underlying factor, rain falling on cornfields and swamps in Iowa. In this case you might plausibly make a decision based on the supposition that corn prices and mosquitoes (in Iowa) will be negatively correlated in the future.

What if the swamp were in Louisiana, but El Niño causes higher rainfall in both Iowa cornfields and Louisiana swamps? Again, the same underlying factor—El Niño—affects both corn prices and mosquitoes so you might plausibly make a decision based on the supposition that corn prices and mosquitoes (in Louisiana) will be negatively correlated in the future. But in most cases, it is better to look at the underlying factor directly (El Niño) rather than indirectly through its effects on other variables (such as corn prices and mosquitoes). However, sometimes the underlying factor cannot be observed, so indirect correlations are all that are available.

The point is that you should not take observed correlations at face value. You must use your judgment to decide whether the association between the variables is due to common underlying causes or just coincidence. Coincidental correlations are not likely to be reliable as predictors of future correlation.

In cases where volatility can be quantified, correlation can be quantified. If it can, judging the degree of correlation can make a crucial difference in making good risk decisions. If two things are perfectly correlated, their correlation is 1.0 and they move in perfect lockstep. If one is up, the other is up in the same proportion.

If two things are uncorrelated, their correlation is zero and there is no relationship at all between the movements of one and the movements of the other. If one is up, the other is just as likely to be up as down.

Most correlations involved in real problems lie somewhere between the extremes of –1 and 1. The correlation between rainfall in the swamp and mosquitoes in your backyard could be .6, meaning that there is a strong tendency, but not a certainty, that higher rainfall means more mosquitoes. Why? Because mosquitoes are affected not just by rainfall but by other factors as well, such as the bird population. Even if rainfall is up, mosquitoes might be down because the bird population is up. There could be other unknown factors at work as well, so that taking both rainfall and bird population into account still leaves you with an imperfect predictor of mosquito levels.

Earlier we said that your portfolio of two volatile stocks will probably be less volatile than a portfolio of either stock by itself. We can quantify this effect by applying the concepts of volatility and correlation. We start by asking you to quantify your beliefs about the volatility of each stock and the correlation between them. Remember that you are the risk manager, so it is only your beliefs about the future that matter. Statisticians and finance experts might give you useful information about the historical volatilities and correlation between the stocks or about the economic factors affecting the stocks, but you have to decide how to use this information in forming your own beliefs. You might decide that the experts' historical and economic analyses have been overtaken by events (such as the economic collapse of Russia), leading you to believe that the future volatilities of each stock and the correlation between the stocks will be higher than experts or history would suggest. So you take their estimates, apply your own judgment, and arrive at beliefs that you are willing to act upon.

Finally returning to our example, suppose that you believe that each stock will have a volatility of 20 (ignore, for now, what this means) and that the correlation between them will be 0.6. A correlation of .6 implies a strong, but not perfect, tendency for the two stocks to rise and fall together. Also suppose that you are trying to decide whether to put all your money in only one stock or invest half in one stock and half in the other. By using the mathematics of volatility and correlation, you would compute that the volatility of the two-stock portfolio will be 17.9. In other words, holding the two-stock portfolio, with a volatility of 17.9, would be somewhat less than the volatility of 20 for holding either stock by itself.

Now suppose that you believe the values of the two stocks will be unrelated to each other in the future. If one goes up, the other will be just as likely to go down as up. Your beliefs imply a correlation of zero between the stocks. A correlation of zero means that the two-stock portfolio will have a volatility of 14.1, significantly less than the volatility of 20 for either stock by itself.

Finally, suppose that you believe that the values of the two stocks always, without exception, moved in opposite directions by the same amount. What was good for one stock was always equally bad for the other. Your beliefs imply a correlation of –1.0 between the stocks. A perfect negative correlation means that the two-stock portfolio would have a volatility of zero—gains in one stock will always cancel losses in the other.

This example shows the potentially powerful effects of correlations on volatility. If you are measuring risk by using volatility, you also have to assess your beliefs about correlation.

Chapter 4

FUNDAMENTAL STRATEGIES FOR MANAGING RISKS

You are faced with a risky situation. You are the decision maker. What are you going to do? Whatever risks you face, whatever strategy you chose, you will be doing one or more of the following:

- Identifying
- Quantifying
- Preventing
- Creating
- Buying and selling
- Diversifying
- Concentrating
- Hedging
- Leveraging
- Insuring

These are the fundamental strategies for managing risks. Any action that affects your risk exposure involves one or more of these strategies. Having them in mind when you approach a risk problem may save you time and may prevent you from overlooking an important risk or an effective action to deal with it.

IDENTIFYING THE RISKS THAT YOU FACE

It is hard to manage a risk if you do not know that it is there. Because identifying risks is easier if you have some idea of what you are looking for, knowing something about common categories of risk can give you an important advantage. If you are trying to spot rare birds, you need to know which types of birds are rare, what they look like, and where they are mostly likely to live. And if you have the good luck to find a bird that has never been seen by anyone before, how will you know it unless you can compare it to the list of birds already identified and categorized? As Spinoza said, "Chance favors the prepared mind."

Unfortunately, the categorization of risk is not as advanced or as precise as it is in biology where millions of plants and animals are already identified and slotted into thousands of distinct categories that are generally accepted by all scientists. One difficulty in categorizing risks is that the definition of "risk" is directly linked to the definition of "bad outcome," which is sometimes ambiguous and subjective (Chapters 1 and 2). Another difficulty is simply that knowledge of some types of risk has evolved within different guilds of experts who are isolated from each other. Each guild has developed its own perspective, practices, and language, which makes communication and common understanding difficult. For example, despite their mutual dependence on statistics, insurance actuaries and financial risk managers have had little professional contact with one another, just as plumbers and car mechanics have had little professional contact with one another despite their mutual dependence on mechanical engineering. In the case of plumbers and car mechanics, this isolation does not matter very much. Neither makes daily reference to the Navier Stokes equations that describe fluid flow in both car engines and in toilets. In the case of insurance actuaries and financial risk managers, it is only recently that they have begun to cooperate on risk management techniques that combine elements of both the insurance markets and financial markets, such as bonds whose payments are linked to the occurrence of natural catastrophes. When they finally started talking to each other, they were able to create something new and useful for the world.

In the absence of a universal and comprehensive system for categorizing all risks, you can try to place your particular risk situation in a context that many decision makers have faced before and hope that your predecessors have already identified and categorized most of the risks that you will be facing. If they have, you can get a head start by applying some of their experience to your problem rather than starting from scratch. For example, borrowing from the experience of others is likely to be possible if your risks are medical (deciding whether to have elective surgery), political (deciding whether to run for governor), meteorological (deciding whether to plant corn or soybeans this year), or geological (deciding whether to build your house near a fault zone). In each of these disciplines, a wealth of risk information is available for several types of preidentified risks. Although none of it is likely to fit your situation exactly, you would be foolish to ignore it and you will probably make better decisions by applying it with good judgment. By categorizing different risks, you can often break a complex, amorphous blob of risks into smaller and simpler manageable parts.

In Chapter 6, we identify the major categories of risk facing a business enterprise.

QUANTIFYING THE RISKS YOU FACE

We discussed the quantification of risks in Chapters 1, 2, and 3 when we introduced decision trees and putting numbers on your beliefs about the probability of uncertain events and the pleasure or pain you would feel if the events were to happen. We then discussed volatility and correlation measures that could be useful in quantifying some kinds of risks in practical situations.

In trying to quantify risks, however imperfectly, you are forced to think harder and more concretely about your risk exposure than if you relied solely on hazy intuition or gut feel. Having quantified your risks, you can take rationally calculated actions that are more closely tailored to your particular situation and therefore more effective in moving you closer to your desired risk profile. You can compare the magnitude of one risk against the magnitude of another risk and decide how to trade some of one risk for some of the other. You can also gauge how much risk you are taking in total, even if you are taking many different types of risk.

PREVENTING RISKS

The most obvious risk management strategy is to prevent or avoid unwanted risks. Don't go for a midnight walk in a high-crime neighborhood. Don't build your house on a flood plain. Don't go cliff diving in Acapulco. Don't invest your life savings in Perpetual Motion Incorporated at the urging of a stranger on the phone. Have your brakes checked before you go on a road trip through the Rocky Mountains. The better you are at identifying and quantifying risks, the better you will be at preventing or avoiding unwanted risks. You should not voluntarily take a risk that has no potential to contribute to your welfare.

CREATING RISKS

Just as you try to prevent or avoid unwanted risks, you want to create desirable risks. Desirable risks are those embedded in attractive opportunities where you believe that the potential gain outweighs the risks. Of course, it would be ideal if you could achieve a gain without taking any risk, but life usually does not work that way. Opportunities usually come with risks attached. As the saying goes, "Nothing ventured, nothing gained."

Many people think that the goal of risk management is to eliminate risk—to be as cautious as possible. Not so. The goal of risk management is to achieve the best possible balance of opportunity and risk. Sometimes achieving this balance means exposing yourself to new risks in order to take advantage of attractive opportunities.

BUYING OR SELLING RISKS

If you cannot prevent or avoid an unwanted risk, you may be able to sell it. If you cannot create a desired risk, you may be able to buy it. Suppose that you are very worried about your house being swept away in a flood. Even though you are not able to prevent a flood, you may be able to sell your house to someone who is not as worried about floods as you are. The selling price may not be what you hoped for, but you can rid yourself of the entire risk. If you are thrilled by the prospect of climbing Mount Everest, you can buy a place on an expedition—buying a risk of death in order to gain a chance for glory. Of course, we don't usually think of buying a risk in order to have the risk, but of buying the opportunity and accepting the risk that comes with it. But since we are concerned about risk management, it is useful to use this seemingly backward phrase to keep our terms consistent.

DIVERSIFYING RISKS

You diversify risk when you don't put all your eggs in one basket. Diversification is a very powerful way to manage risks and it has been practiced for centuries, in one form or another. The power of diversification is that it can, in many cases, reduce risk substantially without reducing the expected gain, thus making diversification one of the few free lunches available in life.

For example, in situations where outcomes are not highly correlated with each other, diversification can provide substantial risk reduction benefits. Many believe that the stock market fits this description reasonably well and therefore that diversification of stock holdings is a good idea. As we show in

Chapter 6, dividing your portfolio among 20 or 30 or more stocks substantially reduces the volatility of portfolio returns without sacrificing expected portfolio returns.

To understand the effects of diversification, consider the following example. Imagine that you are the ruler of a colonial empire. You have amassed a large cache of gold, worth $100 million, in a faraway colony and must transport it across a vast ocean to bring it home. All the gold would fit in a single ship, but you have many ships available. All the ships will be sailing anyway, whether or not they carry any of the gold, so there is no extra shipping cost if you use more than one ship for the gold. You know from experience that two out of every ten ships has been lost making the dangerous crossing so you assign a 20 percent probability to any single ship sinking. You face a risk decision: should you put all your gold in one ship or spread it across two ships? Let's look at the decision tree for each strategy as shown in Figure 4.1.

We are assuming that the fate of each ship is independent of the fate of the other. Losing one ship makes it no more or less likely that we will lose the other ship. They won't be lost in the same storm, for example. In other words, the fates of the ships are not *correlated* with each other. This lack of correlation is what allows diversification to work.

If you put all the gold on one ship, there is a 20 percent chance of losing it all and an 80 percent chance of saving it all. If you put $50 million of gold into each of two ships, there is a 4 percent chance of losing both ships (a $100 million loss), a 32 percent

Figure 4.1
One Ship or Two? Possible Outcomes

	SHIPS SUNK	PROBABILITY	VALUE
Put all gold in one ship — Safe 80%	0	80%	$100
Sunk 20%	1	20% 100%	$0

	SHIPS SUNK	PROBABILITY	VALUE
Ship 2 Safe 80%	0	64%	$100
Ship 1 Safe 80% / Sunk 20%	1	16%	$50
Sunk 20% / Safe 80%	1	16%	$50
Sunk 20%	2	4% 100%	$0

chance of losing one ship and saving one ship (a $50 million loss), and a 64 percent chance of saving both ships (no loss).

Which strategy do you prefer? By diversifying, the two-ship strategy dramatically reduces the chance of losing $100 million (from 20 percent to 4 percent) but also reduces the probability of saving it all (from

80 percent to 64 percent). Both strategies produce the same "expected" value of $80 million of the gold being saved, meaning that if you repeated each strategy 1,000 times you would, on average, save $80 million of the gold using either strategy. Unfortunately, you won't be doing this 1,000 times. You have only one shot, and the outcome is very uncertain. If you are risk averse, you might be more anxious to avoid disaster than to hold out for the best possible outcome.

To know if and to what degree you are risk averse, we need to assess your utility for wealth in this situation. Since we went through a similar process in an earlier example, we won't go through all the steps here. Assume that we have your utility function for wealth and use it to complete your decision tree as shown in Figure 4.2.

Now we now know that the diversifying two-ship strategy is better, for you, than the go-for-broke, one-ship strategy. We know this because the two-ship strategy offers you a higher expected utility. Given your probability assessments and preferences, the likely pain of losing everything was more important than the likely pleasure of preserving everything.

Two ships provide some diversification, but four ships would provide even more. The probability of losing all the gold is reduced from 4 percent (.2 × .2) with two ships to 0.16 percent with four ships (.2 × .2 × .2 × .2). But the four-ship strategy also reduces the chance of saving all the gold from 64 percent (.8 × .8) with two ships to 41 percent (.8 × .8 × .8 × .8) with four ships. Even though it gives you less than a 50–50 chance of saving all the gold, would a four-ship strategy be a better decision for you than the

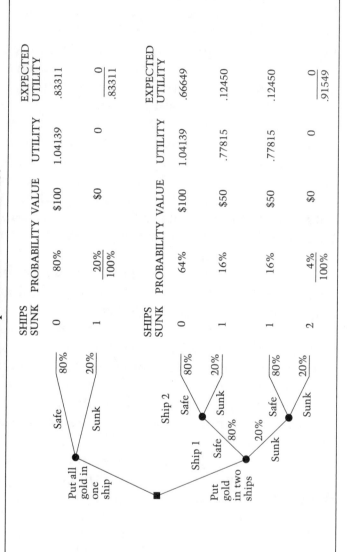

Figure 4.2
One Ship or Two? Decision Tree

	SHIPS SUNK	PROBABILITY	VALUE	UTILITY	EXPECTED UTILITY
	0	80%	$100	1.04139	.83311
	1	20%	$0	0	0
		100%			.83311

	SHIPS SUNK	PROBABILITY	VALUE	UTILITY	EXPECTED UTILITY
	0	64%	$100	1.04139	.66649
	1	16%	$50	.77815	.12450
	1	16%	$50	.77815	.12450
	2	4%	$0	0	0
		100%			.91549

two-ship strategy? Yes, it would. The expected utility of a four-ship strategy is higher than that of the two-ship strategy. In fact, if diversification were free (as we have assumed here), you would send as many ships as you had. In real life, diversification is usually not free and at some point further diversification would not be worth the extra cost.

CONCENTRATING RISKS

You concentrate risk when you put all your eggs in one basket and according to Bernard Baruch, "you watch the basket." Why would you ever want to concentrate risk when diversifying risk is supposed to be such a good thing? One such case is when you would rather preserve the possibility of extremely good outcomes than reduce the probabilities of very bad outcomes. Another case is when you can actually increase the odds of good outcomes by focusing your attention and effort on managing a few opportunities rather than spreading yourself too thin managing many opportunities. We are assuming that you have some positive influence over the outcomes. If you do not, you should not overlook the probable benefits of diversifying.

For example, a large investor who is actively involved in the management of a company has influence over what the company does and how successful it will be. The large investor may be better off putting a substantial fraction of his portfolio in that company in order to gain maximum influence on management and to focus his limited time on working with the company. A small investor has no such influence and would gain nothing by putting a large fraction of his wealth in that company.

HEDGING RISKS

Hedging is another way of dealing with unwanted risks. You hedge when you acquire a new risk that exactly offsets the unwanted risk, leaving you with no risk. Since each outcome of the hedge *exactly* offsets *each* outcome of the unwanted risk, the net outcome is always zero. This is called a *perfect* hedge and is just as effective as selling the risk.

Consider this simple example of a perfect hedge. The Knicks are playing the Celtics in a basketball game. You have bet $100 on the Knicks winning. But now you are having second thoughts about the wisdom of betting on this game. You hedge your unwanted bet on the Knicks by placing another bet of $100 on the Celtics. This strategy works because if the Knicks win, the Celtics *must* lose and vice versa. If the Knicks win, you win $100 on the Knicks bet and lose $100 on the Celtics bet, so the net outcome is zero. If the Celtics win, you win $100 on the Celtics bet and lose $100 on the Knicks bet. Again, the net outcome is zero. Your perfectly hedged bet is just like no bet at all.

Unfortunately, it is not easy to find a costless, perfect hedge. Most real hedges either cost something to acquire or do not exactly hedge you against all outcomes. As professional risk managers like to say, "The only perfect hedge is in a Japanese garden." Consider another sports betting example. The Rangers are playing the Blackhawks in a hockey game. You have bet $100 on the Rangers to *win*. But you are having second thoughts about the wisdom of betting on this game, so you try to hedge your unwanted bet by betting $100 on the Blackhawks to *win*. The $100 payoff from a Rangers win is offset by the $100 loss from the Blackhawks loss, or vice versa if the Blackhawks win and the Rangers lose. So far so good. You have perfectly hedged all outcomes where one team wins and the other loses (just as in the basketball game example). Unfortunately, because hockey games can end in *ties*, your "hedge" has created a possible outcome where you lose $200 (because neither team wins), *twice* the possible loss from your original bet. Hedges that actually *increase* your loss potential in some scenarios are called "Texas hedges," for reasons that are unclear to me and possibly insulting to Texans.

"Hedge" is the second most dangerous word in risk management (leverage takes first place, see next section). Lulled into a false sense of security by thinking themselves hedged, institutions have unwittingly taken on huge risks that proved to be disastrous. When you avoid or sell a risk, it is gone. When you hedge a risk, maybe it is gone and maybe it is not. This potential pitfall of hedging does not mean that you should never hedge your bets—many hedges work very well. But it does mean you must be very, very careful when considering a hedge to make sure that it won't ever blow up in your face.

LEVERAGING RISK

When you leverage a risk, you magnify all of its potential outcomes, good and bad. If you can lift a 500-pound rock with a 3-foot lever, you can use the same force to lift a 1,000-pound rock with a 6-foot lever. A 6-foot lever has twice the lifting power of a 3-foot lever. It also hits you in the face twice as hard if you lose your grip at the wrong moment.

Although leverage may be used in other areas of risk management, it is in finance that leverage displays its truly awesome power and danger. In finance, the simplest way to create leverage is to borrow money to buy a risky asset. Suppose you have $1 million in your wallet and you want to buy a stock. One way is to simply invest $1 million of your own money to buy $1 million of the stock. Another way is to *leverage* your investment by investing $1 million of your own money and borrowing another $1 million from the bank in order to buy $2 million of the stock. To keep things simple, let's assume that you believe that there are only two possible outcomes for the stock: It will increase in value by 50 percent over the next year with 70 percent probability or it will lose 25 percent of its value with 30 percent probability. Let's compare the possible outcomes of the leveraged strategy with the unleveraged strategy (see Figure 4.3).

The leveraged strategy offers a much higher upside than the unleveraged strategy (92 percent return vs. 50 percent) but also a much greater downside (losing 58 percent of the original investment vs. 25 percent).

Figure 4.3
Leveraged Stock Investment

	Stock Gains 50% (70% Probability)	Stock Loses 25% (30% Probability)
Unleveraged Strategy		
Year-end portfolio value	($1 million × 1.5) = $1.5 million	($1 million × .75) = $.75 million
Repay loan	$0 × 108% = $0 million	$0 × 108% = $0 million
Net value of portfolio	$1.5 million − 0 = $1.5 million	$.75 million − 0 = $.75 million
Return on investment	($1.5 million − $1million)/$1 million = 50%	($.75 million − $1 million)/ $1 million = −25%
Leveraged Strategy		
Year-end portfolio value	($2 million × 1.5) = $3 million	($2 million × .75) = $1.5 million
Repay loan	$1 × 108% = $1.08 million	$1 × 108% = $1.08 million
Net value of portfolio	$3 million − $1.08 million = $1.92 million	$1.5 million − $1.08 million = $.42 million
Return on investment	($1.92 million − $1 million)/$1 million = 92%	($.42 million − $1 million)/ $1 million = −58%

Leverage has magnified both the upside and downside of the investment. Leverage doubled the size of your stock portfolio and therefore doubled the potential gains and losses on that portfolio. But the lender does not share in those gains or losses—they are all yours. The lender gets his principal back and is paid the same interest rate no matter what happens to the asset.

One reason why leverage is so popular in finance is that companies and individuals often have *limited liability*, which means that they cannot lose more than their original investment. By using leverage and limited liability, you can increase your potential gains but *not* increase the maximum amount you could lose. However, the *probability* that you will lose all of your investment increases as you increase your leverage. Limited liability shifts some of your risk to the lender, because in some scenarios you will not have enough money to pay back the full amount of the principal and interest. Of course, lenders understand leverage and they try to compensate for the added risk by charging you a higher interest rate on the loan and by limiting the amount of leverage you can take.

INSURING THE RISK

Everyone is familiar with insurance. When you *insure* a risk, you pay a premium to an insurer who will pay you money *if and only if* a loss event occurs. If a loss event occurs, the payment from the insurer will cover all or part of your loss. If the loss is not financial, the insurance payment may compensate, to some degree, for pain and suffering. If no loss event occurs, the insurer pays you nothing and *in hindsight* it might seem that you paid an insurance premium for nothing. Of course, you *did* get something for your money—*protection against a bad outcome* that allowed you to sleep better at night. If you bought fire insurance on your house and it did not burn down, you probably don't regret paying that insurance premium.

The amount and variety of insurance policies that can be purchased is staggering. Life insurance, car insurance, health insurance, flood insurance, liability insurance—the list goes on and on. Huge amounts of risk are transferred from those who don't want it to those who think they can manage it at a profit.

Despite this abundance of insurance, many risks remain uninsured. We all know from personal experience that insurance rarely covers all losses that we are worried about. Sometimes we know this before we buy a policy and sometimes we find out later when we try to collect. Just as there are few perfect hedges, there are few perfect insurance policies. In order to write an insurance policy, insurers must convince themselves that the risk is identifiable, quantifiable, manageable, and saleable at a profit. Running an insurance company is largely an exercise in risk management and in marketing.

Why can an insurance company handle risks that everyone else wants to get rid of? Because, above all else, an insurance company can *diversify* away much of the risk. By pooling hundreds, thousands, or millions of individual risks, the insurance company hopes to create a highly diversified portfolio. If it does, the company will be able to predict the loss on its pooled portfolio with a high degree of confidence and be able to price its policies to cover that predictable loss and be left with a predictable profit. In effect, a specialized user of one tool of risk management (diversification) can create another risk management tool that can be used by others (insurance). This strategy works very well as long as the insurance company actually achieves a diversified portfolio. If it does not, too many bad things may happen at one time, creating losses much greater than expected.

One or more of these fundamental strategies for managing risks (identifying, quantifying, preventing, creating, buying and selling, diversifying, concentrating, hedging, leveraging, and insuring) will be applicable in nearly every risky situation. When you are faced with a new risk problem that requires action, running down this list might help you find an appropriate strategy more easily and quickly.

Chapter 5

THE ENEMY WITHIN

In previous chapters we worked through an idealized way to manage risks which in theory could allow you to find the best possible decision to make when confronted with an uncertain situation. All you had to do was structure your problem as a decision tree, assess your beliefs about the probabilities of the uncertain outcomes, assess your preferences for those outcomes, and do the math. We went on to discuss some of the difficulties of applying our idealized framework to complex, real-life situations and described some examples of shortcuts and approximations that hopefully could lead you to better decisions than you could make with gut feel alone.

But shortcuts and approximations are not the only sources of error in analyzing and managing risks. At the risk of undermining your newly acquired confidence in the power of pure logic, we must point out some common obstacles to rational decision making that arise from the curious ways that human beings actually think. Of course, we do not even expect to be rational in some spheres of life, such as romance or religion. In romance, when logic conflicts with love, love wins and in religion, when logic conflicts with faith, faith wins. But in many other spheres of life, we want to be rational and try very hard to be rational. Despite these good intentions, we all behave, at times, in predictable ways that may not be rational.

In numerous scientific papers published since 1970, Amos Tversky and Daniel Kahneman were among the first scholars to recognize that there are many obstacles to rational decision making about risks that are deeply rooted in human psychology. It is not just a problem of poor information, too little time to think, or making mistakes in doing the math that logic requires. If it were, better information and faster computers would progressively bring us closer and closer to rational decisions. Unfortunately, something else is at work here—human nature. There are particular patterns in our decision making behavior that appear again and again—habits of mind that interfere with our ability to make rational risk decisions.

Many of the psychological biases described in the following sections are drawn from the work of Tversky and Kahneman.

OVERCONFIDENCE

One common trait that can lead to poor decisions is *overconfidence*. We usually underestimate the range of possible outcomes from uncertain events. We assume that the more extreme possibilities, both good and bad, are much less likely than they really are so we focus on a spectrum of possibilities that is far too narrow. Therefore, we are too often surprised by outcomes that fall outside the range of possibilities that we had considered when making the decision.

A friend told me of an experiment he saw conducted at a seminar. The speaker showed the audience a jar filled with paper clips and asked each person in the audience to write down their high and low estimates for the number of paper clips in the jar. They were to pick a high estimate that they believed had a 99 percent probability of being greater than the actual number of paper clips and a low estimate that they believed had a 99 percent chance of being less than the actual number of paper clips. In other words, there should be only a 2 percent probability that the actual number fell outside their estimated ranges. After they had written down their estimated ranges, she announced the actual number of paper clips in the jar and asked all those whose estimated range had contained the actual number of paper clips to raise their hands. If the people in the audience had a realistic view of the range of possible outcomes, nearly all of them would have raised their hands (98 percent), but in fact only a third of the audience raised their hands. Most people in the audience had grossly underestimated the range of possible outcomes. The speaker remarked that she had done this experiment with many audiences and the performance of every audience had been equally dismal.

The consequences of overconfidence can be to take excessive risks or to pass up attractive opportunities. As it happens, we are more likely to underestimate the risks rather than the opportunities because of another habit of mind that can lead us astray—optimism.

OPTIMISM

Excessive *optimism* leads us to expect results that are better than what a dispassionate assessment of the odds would justify. Nearly all of us believe we are better-than-average drivers but only half of us really are. Not only that, most of us exaggerate our ability to control events and we underestimate the probabilities of bad outcomes that are, in fact, out of our control. "Other people who are bad drivers will probably have accidents, but not with *me.*" Or, "There is not a chance in a million that I will die because of an asteroid hitting the earth." Actually, the odds are about 1 in 10,000 during an average person's lifetime, which makes death by asteroid more likely than death by air travel, according to Duncan Steel, a scientist and former head of Australia's asteroid search effort (*The Guardian* [Manchester], September 16, 2000). Perhaps we underestimate the odds because we assume that the National Aeronautics and Space Administration has this sort of thing under control. They don't.

The consequences of excessive optimism can be to take excessive risks (particularly in situations where we think we are in control) or to pursue opportunities with poor prospects for high reward.

HINDSIGHT

Why are we so often overconfident and overoptimistic? Don't we learn from experience? Shouldn't those too-frequent surprises and disappointments teach us to be more realistic in our assessment of probabilities? Not necessarily, because another of our failings is faulty *hindsight.* We misinterpret past events. We cannot accurately reconstruct what we thought about the probability of an event *before* that event occurred. Once we know what happened, we honestly believe that we assigned a much higher probability to the event than we actually did at the time. Events that we had considered highly unlikely or had not even imagined, we now claim to have forecast as likely or even inevitable. If our team loses, we say we saw it coming even though before the game we believed victory was ours. If one of our stocks falls abruptly, we kick ourselves for not acting on our (nonexistent) hunch that things were going badly.

This tendency to rewrite history to gloss over our surprises and disappointments makes it difficult for us to recognize the errors produced by our overconfidence and overoptimism. So the habits continue.

PATTERN SEEKING

Most people are very reluctant to believe that a sequence of events is random or unexplainable. We prefer order to chaos and crave the comfort of predictable cause-and-effect explanations. As Einstein said, "God does not play dice with the universe." We are adept at finding patterns, even when they are not there. We see a man in the Moon, a Big Dipper in the night sky, and canals constructed by intelligent life on Mars. We love to weave conspiracy theories to explain unexpected and baffling political events. If there had been a conspiracy, events were being orchestrated by someone and could have been prevented if only the right people had been in control and the right levers had been pulled. Conspiracy theorists instinctively reject the more likely explanation that the events were just accidental outcomes of a process that no one fully understands or controls. An example from the financial world is the eagerness of many people to assume that a mutual fund manager with five years of above-average performance has above-average skill that will enable him to outperform the averages over the next five years. In fact, a five-year track record tells us little about how the manager will do over the next five years. We see a pattern that is not there.

OVERCOMPENSATION

We overcompensate when our success in reducing one type of risk tempts us into behavior that causes us to take too much of other types of risk, leaving us in a riskier situation than we intended. Suppose you try to reduce your risk of dying in a car accident by buying a car that's equipped with antilock brakes. Antilock brakes are a proven technology that can stop your car quickly and can prevent you from skidding out of control on slippery roads. Everything else being equal, you are less likely to die in a car accident if you have antilock brakes, so you believe that you have made a good risk decision. But suppose your higher confidence in the safety of your car causes you to drive faster when the roads are slippery? The danger of your faster driving may more than offset the higher safety provided by your antilock brakes. You intended to reduce your risk but have actually put yourself at greater risk.

MYOPIA

Myopia is another habit that can lead us to make bad decisions about risk. One form of myopia is to look only to the recent past for clues about the future. Suppose you are deciding whether to buy a house in a beautiful river valley. You look around you and see no signs of flooding. The ground is dry, the house does not have watermarks near the dining room ceiling, there are no boats beached on your neighbor's front lawn, and there are no dead cows floating down the river. You ask a passing child if she has ever seen a flood around here. She says no and hurries off to school. Based on this evidence, you think the flood danger is low so you buy the house. A week later, you watch your favorite easy chair float away in a stiff current. If you had looked further back in time before making your decision, you might have discovered that though the river has not flooded in twenty years, it has flooded five times in the last century. Your historical myopia has caused you to make a very poor assessment of the risk of living in your new neighborhood.

Another form of myopia is failing to imagine what might happen beyond the near future. A teenager who is bored with school drops out to work on his car, which he finds much more satisfying. He is ignoring the very likely scenario that his lifetime earnings will be much lower because of his lack of education, impairing his ability to buy cars in the future. For centuries, the Grand Banks was teeming with a seemingly inexhaustible supply of cod and fisherman took as many fish as they could catch. When people finally recognized a future scenario in which the cod could be depleted, it was too late to recover from the overfishing.

It is not that the distant past or future is always relevant to making a decision; often they are not. But ignoring the distant past or future should be a deliberate judgment rather than an unconscious habit.

INERTIA

Doing nothing can be a valid alternative, but it should get no more weight than it deserves when compared to other alternatives. But more often than we should, we feel safer by doing nothing than by doing something. Like deer frozen in the headlights, we fail to act in time. Perhaps, like the scientist, we are waiting for more information to resolve our doubts, but we wait too long. Perhaps we are waiting for a better set of alternatives to materialize or for the problem to go away by itself, but we wait too long.

Or perhaps we know that we will regret an action that turns out badly more than we will regret an inaction that turns out even worse. Sins of commission are likely to be regretted (and criticized) more than sins of omission. For example, many people will not vaccinate a child against a deadly disease if one of the remotely possible side effects of the vaccine is death, even though the probability of the child dying is much higher without the vaccine. Taking an action, vaccinating the child, that results in the child's death will be regretted much more than inaction, not vaccinating the child, that results in the child dying from the disease. They avoid the vaccine even though they greatly increase the child's risk of death.*

COMPLACENCY

Complacency causes us to be unduly comfortable with familiar risks. Driving a car is one of the riskiest things we do in daily life, yet we rarely worry about it unless we have an accident or a narrow escape from an accident. But even then, the greater awareness of risk fades quickly. Driving is such a frequent, familiar activity that we rarely think about its dangers. (And if you are the driver rather than a passenger, you may compound complacency with the overoptimism that comes from the feeling of control that goes with being the driver.) Unless you live in a small town, the television news no longer bothers to report fatal car accidents unless there are an unusually large number of victims, famous victims, or spectacular circumstances, such as a car driving over the edge of the Grand Canyon. Most of us know by now that the fatalities-per-passenger-mile of commercial air travel are much lower than the

*I. Ritov and J. Baron, "Reluctance to Vaccinate: Omission Bias and Ambiguity, "*Journal of Behavioral Decision-Making* (1990).

fatalities-per-passenger-mile of driving. Yet many of us still worry much more about getting on the plane than getting in the car for our death-defying ride to the airport.

As air travel itself becomes commonplace, it too will become so familiar that its dangers won't be given a second thought. But there are many unfamiliar risks remaining for us to worry about. And we do, too much.

One striking example is the intense debate over the danger of synthetic pesticides and chemicals in the food supply. So-called natural foods are presumed to be healthy while synthetic (man-made) pesticides and additives are presumed to be very risky to our health. Natural foods are *familiar*, like apples from grandma's orchard. Unless you are a chemist, synthetic substances are *unfamiliar*—what *is* Alar, anyway? It is a chemical called daminozide, once made by Uniroyal to keep apples from falling from the tree too early. In 1989, Alar's unfamiliarity contributed to public panic and an economic disaster for the apple industry. The news media reported that Alar had been shown to cause cancer in some laboratory mice. An intense media barrage linking an unfamiliar chemical with the word "cancer" was enough to spark a panic. Some cities banned apples from school cafeterias and millions of apples were taken to the dump. Uniroyal took Alar off the market and presumably apples have been falling off the tree a bit early ever since.

But how much risk did Alar actually pose to people who ate apples? Some scientists believe that the research linking Alar to cancer was flawed in a way that exaggerated the risks. I don't know who is right, because I am not a biochemist or medical researcher. The controversy over the risks of synthetic substances is still raging today and we won't resolve that debate here.

But it is fair to ask why synthetic substances such as Alar cause such a fuss when the hazards of commonly used natural substances rarely do. For example, peanuts often contain traces of aflatoxin, a purely "natural" chemical strongly linked to cancer and other serious diseases in humans. Aflatoxin is the result of a fungal infection that may occur in the field or when the peanuts are stored. Careful cultivation, storage, and testing can substantially reduce the concentrations of aflatoxin in peanuts but it is considered impractical to try to reduce it to zero. The Food and Drug Administration permits traces of aflatoxin, up to specified limits, to be in foods sold to humans. I have seen no one picketing the grocery store to have peanut butter removed from the shelves. Why do we have *zero* tolerance for synthetic toxins but *some* tolerance for natural toxins that may be just as dangerous? Is it because we derive false comfort from something that is familiar?

ZEALOTRY

We become zealots when we seize upon only one possible scenario for the future and steadfastly ignore any other possibilities. When we fall in love with a single scenario, we avoid, reject, or distort any information or opinion that conflicts with that scenario.

Zealotry may not be a distinct category because it may involve overconfidence, inertia, complacency, and overcompensation, but it deserves mention because it is so extreme and disturbingly common. We are all too familiar with zealotry in love, politics, and religion. It even appears in the supposedly buttoned-down world of finance when a trader or portfolio manager bets the ranch (either his or someone else's) on one economic scenario. Once the bet is made, the zealous trader forgets any doubts he may have had before he committed himself to the position. Not only has he bet far too much, he will not even change his mind when his scenario fails to unfold and he has experienced losses. He will rejustify his original scenario by somehow distorting or rejecting the contrary data confronting him. Not only will he refuse to sell out and cut his losses, he will bet *more*, unless someone stops him.

Another variant of zealotry found on Wall Street is when a risk manager falls in love with his financial model and forgets about the approximations and simplifying assumptions that it inevitably depends on. His model seems to work initially, perhaps because he has a very good model or more likely it is because he happened to launch it in the calm waters before the rapids around the bend. He is lulled into a false sense of security. He allows risks to accumulate because his model tells him they are well within the bounds of prudence. Then the rapids appear. His model did not assume that there would be rapids. Risks that appeared small now loom very large and it may be too late to take action to bring the risks back to tolerable levels before big losses have occurred.

Even worse, he may be locked into his position and his losses will magnify if the market keeps going against him. Perhaps the buyers and sellers that he needs to unwind his position have gone to the sidelines in panic. Or perhaps he or his masters are unwilling to recognize the losses and have rationalized their inertia by assuring themselves that the markets will soon return to "normal" and the losses will disappear.

We have considered only some of the many ways that we can be persistently illogical when making decisions about risky situations: overconfidence, optimism, revisionist hindsight, pattern seeking, overcompensation, myopia, inertia, complacency, and zealotry. For example, the *opposites* of some of these traits may occasionally cloud our judgment (underconfidence, pessimism, etc.).

We have come full circle. First we laid out a logical risk management method that promised to lead to the *best possible decision* you could make in a risky situation. That decision was fully consistent with your beliefs about the probabilities of the uncertain outcomes and your preferences for those outcomes. You reached the pinnacle of rationality. Adam Smith and Bertrand Russell would be proud of you. Next, we sobered up a bit and admitted that it would often be difficult for you to force an actual risk decision into our ideal model in a way that was both realistic and solvable with the world's available computing power. You had to simplify and cut some corners and hope that you had captured the essence of your problem even if you had to leave full realism behind. But even then you were being rational. You made reasonable and deliberate tradeoffs to do the best that you could do under the circumstances. Then we confronted the quirks of human psychology that could cause you to unknowingly pass up rational decisions *that are within your grasp.*

So after going full circle, have you gotten anywhere at all? Hopefully, yes. You should now have a much better idea of how to reach a rational decision, be better equipped to understand where you might be falling short, and be on guard against unnecessary mistakes.

We should not leave this subject without admitting that we might have been unfairly critical of the human brain. In talking about the "irrational" habits of mind, we were assuming that we had a clear picture of what the best course of action was. We were making judgments about what was in the best interests of the decision maker. Often, those judgments will be correct, as when someone would genuinely regret a decision and would do the rational thing if she knew better. This might be the case, for example, if an unscrupulous person would be able to exploit her irrationality and make her worse off. However, there might be other cases where our definition of rationality is too narrow and the decision maker is actually being rational when measured against a more complex and realistic set of beliefs and preferences. The decision maker is properly weighing factors that we are ignoring.

For example, if we formulate a decision problem under the assumption that utility is determined by money alone, we may be ignoring something else that independently contributes to utility, such as time. The phrase "Time is money" may be true in the sense that wasted time reduces your wealth. However, is it not generally true that "Money is time." When you are on your deathbed, time cannot be purchased at any price. This does not mean that another day of life has infinite utility. If it did, people would never voluntarily risk their life for anything. It also does not mean that time is never traded for money. Many people work at boring jobs just because they need the income. It just means that the increase in utility of having extra money cannot always compensate for the reduction in utility of losing time. If our decision maker views time as directly contributing to her utility as well as money, then her entirely logical decision may look illogical to an observer who is only considering the utility of money.

The point is that we can say someone is being irrational only if we have fully accounted for her actual beliefs and preferences. If we have, and the decision maker fails to do her math properly or holds impossible beliefs, we have the right to chide her for being irrational. But if we project our own beliefs and preferences on the decision maker, we may be the ones being irrational.

Once again, it is only the decision maker's beliefs and preferences that matter for the purpose of judging whether a rational decision is being made. Of course, if the decision maker's decision affects *you*, and you don't agree with her beliefs and preferences, you should try to change her mind or try to remove the decision from her control.

Chapter 6

GROOMING YOU TO BE CEO

By now, you should have nearly enough knowledge of risk management to become the chief executive officer (CEO) of a major corporation. Of course, skill at risk management is not the only qualification for such a lofty position. Some traditionalists may even claim that it is not nearly as important as other qualities such as leadership, business experience, strategic vision, charisma, and a strong network of well-placed people who owe you something.

Nonetheless, in Chapter 7 we will appoint you to a CEO position and see how you do as a strategic risk manager.

CEOs have two broad responsibilities: *business* decisions, such as how to make and sell their firm's product, and *financial* decisions, such as how to raise and invest funds for their firm. Before we plunge you into the raging battle of capitalism, we will view your business and financial responsibilities through the lens of risk management.

Business risks potentially harm a company's ability to produce and sell its products at a profit. A business risk of an auto company might be an increase in the price of the steel that it needs to build its cars. A business risk of a pharmaceutical company might be the loss of a patent on one of its most profitable drugs. Clearly, a company's business risks are highly dependent on which particular businesses the company is in. Uncertainty about wheat prices is important to General Mills but not to General Motors.

Consider the case of an airline. Major business risks for an airline are uncertainties about jet fuel prices, labor costs, the cost and availability of aircraft, the cost and availability of landing slots, the volume of air traffic and the company's market share of that volume, ticket prices, and, of course, flight safety. Some categories could be divided further and a few other categories might be added, but this list should give you an idea of what to look for when identifying business risks. The CEO must see that these risks are identified, weighed, and managed. Remember that to manage risks is not to minimize them but to balance them against the potential rewards.

Financial risks potentially harm the company's ability to raise sufficient funding at a reasonable cost and to make financial investments that yield an adequate return. A financial risk for a young company might be running out of cash to finance its rapidly expanding operations. A financial risk for a multinational corporation might be a loss on its foreign currency assets due to a devaluation in an emerging market country.

Although we assume that business risks and financial risks are distinct categories, we cannot assume that they do not affect one another. One of your most important jobs as CEO is to know how your business risks and your financial risks combine to create the aggregate risk profile of your firm.

As an example, developing an oil field is a strategic investment and major risk for an oil company. Even for a large oil company, the costs and risks of tapping the field may be uncomfortably high. Business risks include the future price of oil and technical problems that could balloon the costs of pumping and transporting the oil. Financial risks include the cost and availability of financing for the project. In addition, these risks may affect one another. An increase in the volatility of oil prices might cause prospective lenders and investors to raise the costs of financing to cover the higher risk that they are being asked to take. Depending on the method of financing, a future increase in market interest rates could raise interest costs and reduce the profitability of the project over time. Finally, the impact of this project on the oil company's total portfolio of risk must be considered. Does the company already have too much oil price risk? Is it already overexposed to changes in interest rates? Or is the company overcapitalized relative to its total risk profile? If so, some of the excess capital might be liberated to finance part of the new project. All of these risks, both business and financial, should be considered together and managed together to achieve the best possible balance of risk and return for the company as a whole. Which risks should the company take or acquire and which risks should it shed or transform?

Now, as never before, many tools are available to add, subtract, and transform risks. A well-managed company does not have to take unnecessary or unrewarding risks nor does it have to pass up attractive opportunities simply because they come with unwanted risks. Strategic risk management is now a competitive advantage and is becoming a competitive necessity.

From here on, we concentrate on the financial side because that is where the formal discipline of modern risk management began and where, admittedly, the method can be pushed the furthest before running out of reasonable assumptions that lead to solvable problems.

A RISK MANAGEMENT FRAMEWORK FOR YOUR FINANCIAL DECISIONS

Risk managers in the world of finance have developed their own simplifying views of reality. None are believed to be strictly true by any sensible person, but many have proved useful in helping people make better financial decisions. Of course, there are competing views and passionate debates about the merits of each. So what follows are only views, offered as examples, not as dogma.

Defining Financial Risk

We have said that risk means being exposed to a bad outcome and it seems natural to define the financially bad outcome as "losing money." That is a start, but remembering our example in Chapter 1, we know that "losing money" is too vague a term to be useful. We need a *specific and quantifiable* definition of risk (whether it will be a sufficiently *accurate* definition is another question).

The specific and quantifiable definition of risk that is now the reigning favorite in finance is value at risk, or VaR. Value at risk is the potential loss of monetary value that you could suffer within a given time period with no more than a given probability. For example, we could quantify the risk in your million dollar stock portfolio by saying that there is no more than a 1 percent probability that the value of your portfolio could fall by more than $200,000, or 20 percent, over the next year. Your VaR would be

$200,000. If you sold some of your safer stocks and bought an equal value of riskier stocks, your VaR might go up to $300,000, or 30 percent, to reflect the greater risk of your portfolio.

When we first implemented the concept at Bankers Trust in the late 1970s, we used the term "risk capital," not VaR. As other institutions started to use similar methods in later years, the term VaR came into vogue. It doesn't matter what we call it, so we will bow to current fashion and use the term VaR.

Although the concept of VaR is becoming entrenched, there are some lively debates about exactly how to define it in practice. Should we pick a one-year time period or a one-day time period? Should we pick a 1 percent probability level or a 5 percent level? What is the starting point to measure the loss, today's value, the value expected at the end of the chosen time period, or some other value? The list goes on, but we are not trying to turn you into a VaR expert (you are going to be a CEO after all).

Although VaR allows us to quantify financial risk, we gave up some realism to do so. In our ideal world of risk management, your utility function is a fundamental influence on the decisions you should make in uncertain situations. What happened to utility when we adopted VaR as a risk measure? If your utility function is very different from mine, wouldn't you and I have different notions of how to measure risk? If you are much more risk averse than I am, a 1 percent probability of losing more than 20 percent of your stock portfolio over the next year would be much scarier to you than to me. If that were so, VaR proponents would advise you to change your portfolio to reduce the risk (VaR) from 20 percent to some lower number like 10 percent. That advice might be very good, but notice that the advisor did not take into account the particular shape of your personal utility curve, other than to assume that you were risk averse. We gained quantification but lost some realism.

We also lost some realism when we adopted the "no more than 1 percent probability over a year" measure. In our ideal world of risk management, we said that your personal probability beliefs are a fundamental influence on the decisions you should make in uncertain situations. However, by ignoring all possible outcomes having *more* than a 1 percent probability, we have excluded a very large swath of the spectrum of your beliefs about the possible outcomes for stock prices. If you believe that there is only a 30 percent chance of doing better than breaking even, you will probably perceive much more risk than if you believe that there is an 80 percent chance of doing better than breaking even, *even if both situations have the same VaR.* Another potential problem is that VaR does not pick up differences in your beliefs about the probabilities of losses that are *larger* than the VaR. Two portfolios could have the same VaR, yet one could have a 0.5 percent chance of losing more than $600,000 and the other portfolio could have no chance whatever of losing more than $600,000. You would probably regard the first portfolio as riskier than the second portfolio even though both have the same VaR.

If VaR is so flawed as a risk measure, why bother to use it? Because VaR can actually be implemented in practical situations and using VaR is much better than using no risk measure at all, if it is applied with good judgment. Remember that risk management is a combination of risk analysis and risk judgment. Fortunately, the defects of VaR are probably not too serious in many practical situations.

For some (but not all!) financial portfolios, it is reasonable to believe that the possible outcomes can be represented by a bell curve (or normal probability distribution). If you know two particular characteristics of a bell curve, you can describe the whole curve with precision. The first characteristic is the *mean* of the curve, the value that splits the curve into symmetric halves. There is a 50 percent chance that an outcome below the mean will occur and there is a 50 percent chance that an outcome above the mean will occur. There is a higher probability of experiencing outcomes close to the mean than there is of experiencing outcomes far away from the mean. The other defining characteristic of the familiar bell curve is its *standard deviation*, which measures how far the possible outcomes spread out about the mean. If a distribution has a low standard deviation, its possible outcomes are bunched closely about the mean. There is a relatively low probability that outcomes far away from the mean will occur. If a distribution has a high standard deviation, its possible outcomes are spread widely about the mean. There is a relatively high probability that outcomes far away from the mean will occur. In other words, there is a greater degree of uncertainty associated with a higher standard deviation than with a lower standard deviation. Everything else equal, a bell curve portfolio with a high standard of deviation has higher risk than a bell curve portfolio with a low standard deviation (Figure 6.1).

When possible portfolio values are represented by a normal distribution, the VaR of that portfolio is readily computed from the formula that describes the normal curve. In Figure 6.2, the area left of the VaR is called the *left tail* of the distribution. If we are looking for a 1 percent VaR, the left tail of the distribution represents 1 percent of the area under the whole normal curve.

Figure 6.1
Normal Distribution

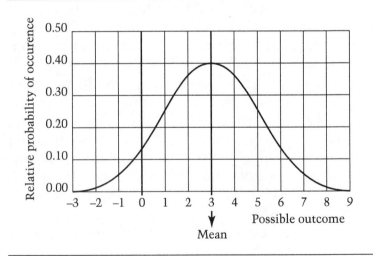

If you happen to believe that a normal distribution describes the probabilities of the possible outcomes for your portfolio, you don't have to worry about the problem, mentioned earlier, of VaR not properly representing the full spectrum of your probability beliefs. Because all the information contained in a normal distribution is captured by its standard deviation and mean, the calculation of VaR does not omit any information about the probability of any outcome, whether above or below the VaR. Your entire belief structure is represented accurately by those two numbers. (However, we are still left with the problem that VaR may not properly account for the shape of your utility curve).

Figure 6.2
Normal Distribution with VaR

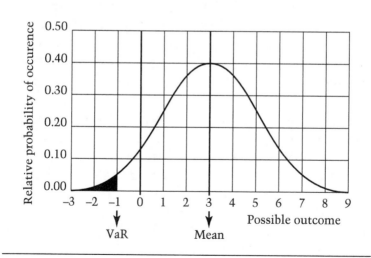

We mention normal distributions because they are often used in finance and because they can easily illustrate some of the principles of portfolio risk management. We do not claim that they *should* always be used in real decisions. If your specific situation leads you to beliefs that do not fit normal distributions closely, you should not use them.

Because normal probability distributions are so convenient, there is a powerful temptation to use them, which inevitably means that they are used too often in situations where they are not really appropriate. One very important example of misuse is when portfolios contain options that do not have the symmetry about the mean assumed by normal distributions. Options are contracts that give the holder the right, but not the obligation, to buy or sell an asset at fixed price in the future, no matter what happens to the price of the asset in the market. Let's say that you bought an option that gives you the right, but not the obligation, to buy ACME stock for $50 per share at the end of the year. You paid $5 per share for your option. ACME stock is now trading at $30 per share. If ACME stock is trading below $50 at the end of the year, you will not buy the stock because you don't want to pay $50 for something that is worth less than $50. If the stock is trading for less than $50, you will have lost $5 on your contract, because you paid $5 for something that turned out to be worthless. But if ACME stock is trading at $80 at the end of the year, you will gladly buy it for $50. Then you will have made $25 on your option contract—the $30 gain minus the $5 cost of your contract. Is the distribution of your possible payoffs "normal"? No, not even close. No matter what happens to ACME stock, the most you can lose is $5, but you could earn $25 if it goes to $80, $35 if it goes to $90, $45 if it goes to $100, and so on, with no upper limit. Your downside possibilities are confined to $5 or less but your upside possibilities are spread over a very wide range. The normal distribution is symmetric but the distribution of payoffs from your option contract is very asymmetric. If you had options mixed in with your stock portfolio, using the assumption that your portfolio returns were normally distributed could give you a very distorted picture of your risk position. By the way, this asymmetry is the reason that options can be so useful in managing risk: They allow you to shape your risk distribution in ways that are otherwise difficult or impossible.

Another example is that for some assets, the normal distribution underestimates the probability of extreme outcomes and thus understates the risk of portfolios containing those assets. For example, there is some statistical evidence that extreme gains or losses occur in stocks more often than would be expected if stock returns were normally distributed. The stock market crash of 1987 may be one such surprise. If this tendency is not taken into account, a volatility calculation (and the VaR) might be too low, causing the risk manager to take more risk than she intended.

So there are potential problems with VaR in general and normal distributions in particular. However, in many situations these problems are not so serious or so unfixable that you would abandon VaR as a measure of financial risk.

Suppose you believe, for whatever reason, that standard deviation of investment returns is a good enough measure of financial risk. If so, you have a powerful tool available that can help you manage those risks. Harry Markowitz, in his landmark paper of 1952, launched the modern era of financial risk management. *

Markowitz assumed that the investor had assessed the expected returns, standard deviations, and correlations of return for a menu of assets being considered for investment. Remember from Chapter 2 that correlation measures the degree to which one asset's value tends to rise and fall in tandem with the value of another asset. Using standard deviation as the measure of risk, Markowitz derived a rigorous mathematical framework for determining the risks and returns of any portfolio constructed of these assets. He also demonstrated how to find the specific portfolio that had the highest expected return for a given amount of risk (or the portfolio that had the lowest risk for a given expected return). If you are risk averse, this framework is very useful for it allows you to eliminate unnecessary risks in your portfolio without sacrificing any expected reward.

Markowitz had created a mathematical explanation and justification for diversification, the most

*"Portfolio Selection," *Journal of Finance,* vol. 7, no. 1 (March 1952), pp. 77–91.

powerful principle of finance. People had known for a long time that spreading wealth across many different risks was likely to be less risky than concentrating wealth in a single risk. But by providing a way to quantify portfolio risks, Markowitz replaced fuzzy intuition with logical analysis. The judgmental leaps required of portfolio managers had become much shorter.

If you are willing to live with all the required assumptions and have all the required data, you now have a powerful tool to manage the risks of your portfolio. For example, suppose you were selecting stocks for a new investment portfolio from a menu of stocks that had identical expected returns and standard deviations but that were not correlated with each other (showing no tendency to move in the same direction, or opposite directions, at the same time). Because all the stocks have identical characteristics, you might be tempted to pick just one of the look-alike stocks and be done with it. But if you have an intuitive feel for the benefits of diversification, you know that you can do better than that by picking several stocks. Just how much better is shown in Figure 6.3.

Picking just one stock gives your portfolio a VaR of 20 percent. Picking two gives a VaR of 14.1 percent, a large reduction in risk. The risk keeps going down as you add more stocks. If you pick 30 stocks, you will have a VaR of 3.7 percent, giving you much less risk and the same expected return as picking just one stock. This is the "free lunch" that diversification provides. The additional risk reduction from diversifying becomes smaller and smaller as you add

Figure 6.3
Diversification If Stocks Are Uncorrelated

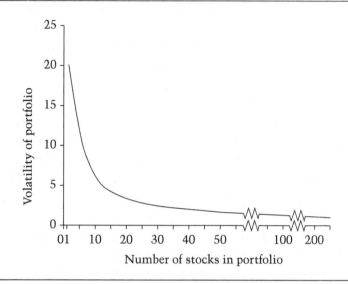

Number of stocks in portfolio

more stocks. However, if the stocks are truly uncorrelated, the risk of the portfolio can be driven to almost zero if you add enough stocks.

Unfortunately, truly uncorrelated stocks are hard to find. The benefits of diversification are smaller when stocks are correlated with each other to some degree, which in reality they usually are. If you have a stock portfolio, you probably experience a sinking feeling when you hear that the Dow is down 300 points, because that probably means that your own portfolio is down also. If we redo our diversification example using a 0.5 correlation rather than a zero correlation, there are still benefits to diversifying, but they are smaller and they reach a lower limit that is determined by their degree of correlation with each other (Figure 6.4).

If all the stocks have a .5 correlation with each other, there is virtually no benefit to diversifying beyond 30 stocks.

The Markowitz framework allows even more complicated portfolios to be analyzed. In the most realistic case, each stock is unique, having a different expected return, standard deviation, and set of correlations than the other stocks. There is no limit to the number of unique stocks that can be considered, in theory.

Using the Markowitz model, you can find the particular portfolio, out of the millions of possible portfolios, that gives you the highest expected return for

Figure 6.4
Diversification If Stocks Are .5 Correlated

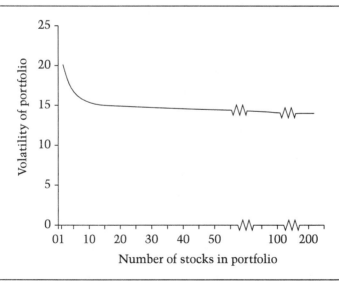

the amount of risk (standard deviation) that you want to take. It is extremely unlikely that you could find this portfolio on your own using just intuition and guesswork. Markowitz created a powerful tool indeed. Most of today's financial risk modeling relies to some degree on variations of the Markowitz technique.

At first glance, it might appear that Markowitz solved all of our risk management issues in one shot. Unfortunately, reality intrudes again. One difficulty is that the size of the problem increases exponentially as the number of stocks increases. A problem with 10 stocks requires you to assess and analyze 55 standard deviations and correlations. A problem with 100 stocks involves 5,050 standard deviations and correlations. A problem with 1,000 stocks, which is a small fraction of the stocks available in the market, involves 500,500 standard deviations and correlations. Where do you get all those expected returns, standard deviations, and correlations? Remember, they must represent *your* beliefs, so you can't just buy them from someone else and use them blindly. Where do you find a computer big enough, fast enough, and cheap enough to use? It is unlikely that the government will lend you a super-computer to manage your personal finances. Fortunately, over the years, many ingenious people have found reasonable simplifying assumptions that cut the Markowitz model down to size and make it a practical real-world tool, when applied with good judgment.

Leaving all the quibbles aside, we have made considerable progress in defining and quantifying financial risk. Even though standard deviation, or other variants of VaR, is at best an approximation of risk, and may sometimes lead us astray, it provides a much better starting point for making risk decisions than unaided intuition and guesswork.

We must enlarge our financial risk framework beyond VaR so we can see what is involved in managing the complexities of risk in specific settings, such as a global financial institution.

A Digression

Before going further, we should recognize that there is an important difference in the nature of the risks faced by individuals and the risks faced by institutions—an institution does not actually experience the consequences of the risks that it takes. An institution merely redistributes the consequences of risk to its individual human constituents—managers, employees, shareholders, citizens, members, clients, beneficiaries, and so on. An oil company is not disappointed when it drills a dry hole, but its human managers, employees, and shareholders may be, to varying degrees. A government is not ashamed when it loses a war, but its human politicians and citizens may be, to varying degrees.

That institutions do not experience risks but people do may seem obvious, but we often forget it and act as if institutions were people. This anthropomorphism is not harmless fun, as it is with Donald Duck, because it can obscure the ultimate effects of institutional decisions on real people. It can also obscure conflicts of interest between the people who make decisions on behalf of the institution and the people who are constituents of the institution.

What does this difference have to do with risk management? It means that risk managers acting on behalf of their institutions may knowingly or unknowingly act on their *personal* risk preferences and transfer inappropriate risks to their institutional constituents. The root cause of many risk management fiascoes has been the conflicting risk preferences of risk takers, their managers, and the constituents of the institution.

For example, some rogue traders who rack up big losses for their firms may be irrationally reckless or incompetent, but others may simply be acting quite rationally to manage their own risks at others' expense. If poorly managed, traders have an *option* that can tempt them to take far more risk than their firm wants them to take. A rogue trader puts a large risk on the books of the firm. The risk position has great profit potential but also great loss potential. In a poorly managed firm, managers may not see this risk position or may not understand it and the rogue trader knows this. If the bet pays off, the firm makes a large profit. The trader is a hero and gets a fat bonus and a promotion. If the bet fails, the firm takes a large loss and the trader is, at most, fired. The trader does not share in the firm's loss even though he shares in the firm's gain. He has a call option on a portion of the profits of the position. Heads, he and the firm win. Tails, the firm loses big money but the trader does not. And to make matters worse, a rogue trader is often eagerly hired by another firm, who is not aware of his behavior, where he can play the same game again. This behavior is unlikely to succeed at a well-managed firm because the trader's managers can see the risks, can understand them, and can control them. Well-managed firms create incentives for traders to behave in the interest of the firm by rewarding them only for *risk-adjusted* profits. If you earn $20 million for the firm and took little risk in doing so and I earn $20 million for the firm but took large risks, you will be rewarded and I will not. Well-managed firms also place limits on how much risk can be taken by any single trader and by the firm as a whole.

So when we talk of the risks facing an institution, we are making the huge assumption that such risk assessments and the decisions flowing from them are appropriate for the institution's rightful human beneficiaries. Sometimes they are, sometimes they are not, and sometimes we simply don't know.

Managing the Financial Risks of Your Company

We will put these complications aside for the moment and consider the example of identifying and categorizing the risks facing a business enterprise. We assume that a business is primarily an economic entity whose principal constituency is its shareholders (this is an assumption beloved by Adam Smith and hated by Karl Marx). This assumption allows us to concentrate on a single measure of risk—financial harm to shareholders. Possible risks are relevant only if they directly or indirectly affect the shareholders' financial interests. But as seen in Chapter 1, even financial harm is too vague a concept to sharply define risk. So for this example, we say that financial harm means "potential losses in the market value of the shareholders' stake in the company."

Most financial risk managers divide financial risks into the following categories:

- Credit risk
- Interest rate risk
- Currency risk
- Commodity risk
- Equity risk
- Operating risk
- Liquidity risk

Credit risk is uncertainty about the ability or willingness of someone to pay back money that they owe someone. Suppose you have a $10,000 U.S. savings bond. You gave the government $10,000 and it promised to pay back your $10,000 later, with interest. In the meantime, the government is using your money to build schools, cruise missiles, or some other public good. Since it is extremely unlikely that the U.S. government will not be willing or able to pay you the money that it owes you, the credit risk on the savings bond is extremely low. But suppose you lent $10,000 to an impoverished friend, believing that there was only a 50–50 chance that he would pay you back. That loan to your friend had a very high credit risk. Today your friend lands a high-paying job. Since your friend now has a higher *ability to pay*, the credit risk on your loan is now much lower than it was yesterday, but still not as low as the credit risk on your savings bond. Banks who lent money to Latin America in the 1970s experienced another kind of credit risk—an *unwillingness to pay* that compounded an impaired ability to pay. The banks eventually lost billions of dollars, but the real tragedy was that many other borrowers who could have used that money to invest in productive ventures were denied credit. A huge opportunity to make the world wealthier was squandered. The informed taking of credit risk is a very important contribution to society, because it allows people with good ideas but not enough money to get the funds that they need to put those ideas into action. Credit risk is also, by far, the biggest risk that financial institutions take and has been the root cause (together with leverage) of most banking failures.

Interest rate risk is uncertainty about the value of fixed income obligations (like loans or bonds) caused by fluctuating yields on similar assets available in the market. If you bought that long-term $10,000 savings bond when savings bonds were paying 5 percent interest and now you can buy an equivalent savings bond (i.e., the same remaining life and the same low credit risk) paying 8 percent, the current value of your old bond is less than the $10,000 you paid for it. Why? Because it only takes $6,250 of the new bond to provide the same interest income ($500 per year) as your old $10,000 bond ($6,250 × .08 = $500). No one would pay more than $6,250 for your old bond if they could get the same income stream, at the same risk, by buying $6,250 of the new bond. (Actually, the math is not quite this simple, but the general idea is the same.) Fluctuating market interest rates put the value of your fixed income assets at risk.

Currency risk is uncertainty about the value of foreign currency assets caused by fluctuating currency rates. Suppose you bought $1,000 worth of pounds, at .70 pounds per dollar to take on your business trip to England. You would now have 700 pounds in your wallet. The next day, the market changes to a new currency rate of .80 pounds per dollar and, coincidentally, you find out that you must cancel your trip. When you go back to the bank to change your pounds into dollars, your company has just suffered a currency loss because you would get only $875 at the new exchange rate (700/.80 = $875). Your company has just lost $125. (If you actually took the trip and spent the pounds in England, you would not have suffered a *spending power* loss on the contents of your wallet because of the exchange rate change. You still have 700 pounds when you land and all prices in pounds, in England, remain unchanged.)

Commodity risk is the uncertainty about the value of holdings of widely used and standardized commodities like gold, silver, and soybeans. If you have 100 ounces of gold in your safe and the price of gold falls by $10 per ounce, you have just lost $1,000. (If you were the CEO of a gold mining company, the uncertain price of gold would probably be classified as a business risk, not a financial risk. But it doesn't really matter as long as you identify and manage the risk.)

Equity risk is the uncertainty about the value of ownership interests in other companies, real estate, or other property. If your company owns 10,000 shares of a high-tech company stock, and the price per share falls by $10, you have just lost $100,000. If your company bought land for a factory site for $8 million and the price of land in that area has fallen by 10 percent, your company has suffered a loss of $800,000.

Operating risk is uncertainty about potential losses caused by mistakes or accidents, criminal acts such as fraud or theft, breakdowns in equipment or technology, and natural disasters. You worry that one of your accountants could skim off $10 million of company funds into his offshore retirement account. You worry that a weakness in your control procedures might allow $5 million of memory chips to be shipped to a thief who is masquerading as a legitimate customer. You worry that an overzealous salesperson might mislead an important customer and get you sued for $50 million, with the potential for treble damages. You worry that a hacker could break in to your company's computer system and wreak havoc. You worry that a severe hurricane could take out 25 percent of your production capacity. These are all operating risks. Their common characteristic is that they don't happen very often, but when they do the consequences can be severe, sometimes catastrophic. Many of these risks can be limited with insurance, which is well suited to Acts of God or other infrequent mishaps beyond the complete control of the insured party. Many of the risks involving the actions of employees can be limited by good management.

There is great danger, though, in being complacent about these risks, especially those with very low probability but very high severity. By definition, they probably won't happen anytime soon, so it is very, very tempting to neglect them. They also involve obscure business processes or remote events that seem peripheral to the exciting day-to-day struggle with market share, strategic direction, capital investment, executive bonuses, and other things that CEOs deem worthy of their attention.

Liquidity risk is uncertainty about the ability to buy or sell something quickly at "fair value." We are going to spend quite a bit of time on this concept because it is the most dangerous and the least understood financial risk. The other risks are simple compared to liquidity risk.

Suppose that you want to sell your house. You have been keeping track of property values in your neighborhood so you know that several houses comparable to yours have sold recently for approximately $250,000. These houses were on the market for no more than six weeks before they sold. You believe that your house is also worth $250,000 and should sell within six weeks or so. You are not alone in this belief because you had the house appraised recently and the appraiser also put a $250,000 value on your house. But now the situation has changed in two ways. First, you have to start your new job in a distant city in six weeks. Second, for no apparent reason, there are very few buyers looking for houses like yours in your neighborhood right now. You believe that this dearth of buyers is only temporary, because nothing in the economy or local housing market has changed. Many of the people who would normally be looking at your house this week may have decided to go on vacation instead. You expect that the buyers will be back soon.

You now face a liquidity risk. Even though the fair value of your house is $250,000, the (hopefully) temporary dearth of buyers leads you to worry that you will not find a buyer at that price within your six-week deadline. You also know that there is a buyer who will pay you $235,000 for your house right now.

You must decide what to do. Sell now at a price below fair value or wait until a buyer appears who is willing to pay fair value?

If you hold out for $250,000, you risk not selling the house for several weeks past your deadline. If that happens, you own a house that you are not living in and you must also pay for housing in your new city. Paying for an empty house is a costly and unpleasant prospect. But that is not all. Holding out for $250,000 exposes you to yet another unpleasant possibility. While you are waiting to find the right buyer, the housing market might actually weaken and the fair value of your house could fall to $220,000. This means that even when the buyers eventually return, they will pay you only $220,000 for your house. Of course, the market could also improve, raising the fair value to $300,000. But you have no idea whether the fair value is going to rise or fall while you are waiting for the right buyer.

You face a liquidity risk because potential buyers at fair value are proving hard to find quickly. What are you going to do? Sell now or wait? If you sell now for $235,000, it costs you $15,000 relative to the current fair value of $250,000. But by selling now, you avoid the costly possibility of owning an empty house and you also avoid the possibility of getting only $220,000 (and losing another $30,000) if the market weakens before you are able to sell. You also give up the possibility of selling later for $300,000 if the market improves. By selling now, you take a certain loss but the future risk is gone. By waiting, you avoid the loss today but the risk of a larger future loss and the opportunity for a future gain remain. This is not a trick question for there is no universally right answer. Only you can decide what is right for you, given your probability beliefs and your preferences for the possible outcomes involved.

Liquidity risk appears in many forms and in many places. If you might have difficulty finding sellers when you need to buy water in the desert (even though you have the cash to buy), you face liquidity risk. If you might have difficulty finding lenders when you need to borrow (even though your credit is good), you face a liquidity risk. If you might have difficulty finding someone to relieve you of a currency risk that you no longer want to take (even though you are willing and able to compensate them fairly for doing so), you face a liquidity risk.

Liquidity risk is very dangerous because it can surprise you at the worst possible time—just when you need to buy or sell. When you can't buy or sell, you can be forced to take risks that you don't want to take and your losses can be much higher than you thought they could be.

Liquidity risk arises because markets don't always work the way economists think they should work—with large numbers of buyers and sellers constantly doing transactions with each other, all day, every day. In the economist's liquid market, if you want to sell, there is always a buyer at a fair price. If you want to buy, there is always a seller at a fair price.

Some real-life markets actually come close to the economist's dream—the market for U.S. Treasury bills, for example. There are thousands of buyers and sellers of treasury bills every day, ranging from individuals to large institutions and dealers. Bills are trading all over the world, 24 hours a day. You can watch the prices move, virtually in real-time, on the internet and other news sources. When you see a price of $97 and want to buy, if you act quickly you will get a price close to $97 and everyone else who is buying at the same time will also get a price close to $97. No one will pay $95 or $99. This is an extremely liquid and fair market (not perfect, but pretty close). So if you buy bills, you are taking very little liquidity risk, because a buyer is highly likely to be there at a fair price when you want to sell. You *are* taking the risk that the fair price of bills may move against you, but if you don't like that risk you can easily and quickly get rid of it at very little cost.

Most other markets are not so reliably friendly as the T-bill market. Some markets are usually very liquid, but occasionally have poor liquidity (dollar/euro currency market). Some markets are moderately liquid at best and often have poor liquidity (houses). Some markets have poor liquidity nearly all the time and terrible liquidity at other times (Guatemalan small cap stocks).

Because liquidity can be so variable within a given market over time and across different markets, it is easy to let yourself be lulled into taking too much liquidity risk. You take a currency risk or an interest rate risk under the assumption that you can easily get rid of all or part of the risk whenever you want to. You find out later that the roller coaster is not as much fun as you thought it would be *and you can't get off.*

One of the fundamental principles of good risk management is having control over your risk positions so that you can get out the door when you need to leave and not leave too much behind. Because liquidity risk takes away some of that control, its presence should curb your appetite for taking on large amounts of other risks such as credit or currency.

An interesting characteristic of liquidity risk is that its consequences are felt through the other risks that you take. Because you took too much liquidity risk, you lost $40 million in your company's currency accounts when you thought the worst case was $20 million, *based on past fluctuations in currency rates in normal markets.* You couldn't cut your losses in the currency markets at $20 million because the market had become illiquid and no one was there to take you out in time. If you could have recognized and quantified liquidity risk ahead of time, you might have seen that there was some chance of losing an *extra* $20 million due to liquidity risk on top of the $20 million you could lose due to typical fluctuations in currency rates in liquid markets. If so, you probably would not have taken such a large currency position and you would not be sitting in front of your board of directors with sweat running down your forehead. But I am being too hard on you. Liquidity risk is devilishly difficult to recognize and quantify. Even so, trying to do so will give you a much better chance of avoiding big trouble.

In a way, liquidity risk is not really a separate risk but simply an additional mechanism for the other risks to bite you.

PUTTING IT TOGETHER

All of the foregoing risk types can be quantified by using VaR (or some other numerical risk measure). Having done so, we can compare one risk to another by comparing their VaRs. We can also combine different risks (using Markowitz math) to see how much risk the company is taking in total. We can test different strategies to see if their expected returns justify their VaRs.

Now you have the basic elements that you need to recognize and quantify the risks of your company. You have a specific, quantifiable measure of risk: VaR, or the probability of losing a given amount of your shareholder's money in a given period of time. You have classified the major categories of financial risk and understand how they arise: credit, interest rate, currency, commodity, equity, operating, and liquidity risks. Although we did not dwell on it, you know that business risks (like uncertain jet fuel prices) can also be categorized and quantified as VaRs (although it is not always easy in practice).

The next step is to put these elements together into a coherent picture of the risk position of your company so that you can make better-informed decisions to guide your company through a dangerous environment.

Chapter 7

THE VIEW FROM
THE CEO'S CHAIR

In Chapter 6 we said that you were going to be appointed the chief executive officer (CEO) of a major corporation and be ultimately responsible for managing all of the risks your corporation faced. You were given the basic elements required to recognize and quantify those risks, both business and financial.

Now you are going to be the CEO of a major financial institution. But before you push any buttons on your fancy rosewood desk, you need to be able to see the forest as well as the trees of your company's risk profile. Fortunately, financial institutions have business risks that are mostly the financial risks we discussed at length in Chapter 6, so we can simplify your job by focusing on financial risks.

So, you are now the CEO of Amalgamated Banking Corporation (ABC), a sprawling global network of banking offices all over the world, including the major financial centers: New York, London, Tokyo, and Hong Kong. You have 35,000 employees, some of whom you have actually met. You have 4,000 corporate and institutional customers, many of whom you have met in pleasant surroundings such as five-star restaurants, gala charity balls, the country club, and your box at the opera. Because you operate in 47 countries and in many different financial businesses, you have the privilege of dealing with 157 different regulatory bodies (many countries thoughtfully provide more than one). For this, your legal staff is truly grateful. For simplicity, we ignore all these pesky regulators (but don't, under any circumstances, do so if you actually become the CEO of a real bank).

ABC is in many financial businesses selling many financial products, but they can all be described as variations of one or more of these fundamental financial activities:

- *Financing.* Moving capital from those who have it to those who need it. A bank finances a borrower by extending a $10 million loan. A venture capitalist finances a new company by investing in $40 million of its newly issued stock.
- *Trading and positioning.* Buying and selling claims on wealth. A brokerage house buys 1,000 shares of Microsoft from me and sells them to you. A commodity trader buys 10,000 pork bellies from you and sells them to me.
- *Advising.* Making decisions on behalf of clients or giving them information and advice that helps them make better decisions for themselves. Your mutual fund uses your money to buy stocks of its choice on your behalf. My investment banker advises me to launch a takeover bid for your company. Your investment banker advises you to turn me down (so you can continue as CEO for the rest of this chapter).
- *Transaction processing.* Storing, safeguarding, reporting, and transferring claims on wealth. A custodian keeps track of which stocks and how much of each stock I own in my investment portfolio. When I sell some shares to you, custodians make sure that the stock is removed from my account and is entered into your

account. We both receive monthly statements describing our holdings and our transactions. We both know where our stocks are and that they are safe from theft or loss.

* *Risk management.* Moving clients closer to their desired risk positions by helping them to shed unwanted risks and to acquire new risks that better fit their preferred balance of risk and return. A derivatives dealer helps me reduce the risk of my investment portfolio by selling me an equity derivatives contract that *increases* in value as stocks go *down* and *decreases* in value as stocks go *up*. Losses on my stocks are fully or partially cancelled out by gains on the derivatives contract and vice versa. Note that you are not only responsible for managing the risks of ABC, but one of the business lines of ABC is selling risk management services to others. Don't let this confuse you; just think of it as any other business for now—a business that creates risks for ABC as a by-product of managing risks for ABC's clients.

You have many talented and highly paid managers to run these businesses every day. Because ABC is a decentralized organization, these managers have considerable freedom to make decisions for their businesses, including hiring and firing, creating new products, dealing with customers, setting prices, and committing ABC to financial obligations. Among your trusted employees are experts on many, many subjects: lawyers, economists, tax people, accountants, information technologists, PR people, security analysts, chefs, chauffeurs, and last, but certainly not least, retooled rocket scientists.

With all this specialized talent on board, you may wonder why you have to know anything at all, let alone risk management. Can't the rocket scientist do the risk management while you confer with the chef? Well, no. There are good reasons why you earn the big bucks as CEO. First, you are the leader and you must tell all these people what broad goals they are working toward and how they will benefit from performing their assigned roles. Second, most experts feel that it is degrading to completely agree with another expert on anything and you will have to choose among their conflicting opinions. Third, if anything goes so seriously wrong that unflattering stories about your company start appearing in the right-hand column on page one of the *Wall Street Journal*, it is *you* who will be roasted by your board, your stockholders, and your 157 regulatory bodies. At that point, it won't help to say that somebody else did it without your knowledge or approval so it wasn't your fault. That just makes it worse. You may not be the only human sacrifice, but you will certainly be among them. Going to the club will never be the same.

So once again, I have put you in a position where you cannot get off the hook. You can and should use the experts around you, but in the end you must decide and you must take the consequences of your decision. Just as a good CEO knows how to use lawyers without being a lawyer, you must know how to use risk management experts without being a risk management expert. To use this amassed expertise requires a coherent view of your company's entire risk profile, how outside events might affect it, and how you can shape it to your company's advantage (even though you, as CEO, cannot possibly know all the details of all the individual risks).

A PORTFOLIO VIEW OF YOUR COMPANY'S RISKS

We start with the simple rule that applies to any company or individual:

(What You Own) minus (What You Owe) equals (What You Can Keep)

What You Own Are Assets

"What You Own," also known as assets, is any and all claims belonging to you that may entitle you to receive something of value now or in the future. These claims can take myriad forms: checking accounts, bonds, stocks, gold, futures contracts, stock options, insurance policies, houses, land, blast furnaces, royalty agreements, employment contracts, magazine subscriptions, and so on.

In some cases, the value to be received is *fixed* (or at least *promised* to be fixed), like a loan repayment. ABC lent ACME Crank Company $10 million, giving ABC a claim that entitles it to receive $10 million plus 8 percent accrued interest, to be paid one year from today. ACME has promised to satisfy this claim. This type of claim is sometimes called a fixed rate loan, note, or bond.

In other cases, the value to be received is *variable*, but defined by a specific formula. A derivatives contract that pays $10 million times the Prime Rate – LIBOR* on 6/30/01 is a variable claim.

Other claims are *contingent*, because the value to be received depends on uncertain future events occurring or not occurring. If your house is destroyed by a hurricane within one year, the insurance company will pay you $300,000. In this case, the uncertain event is beyond anyone's control. In other cases, the uncertain event can be triggered by someone else or by you. For your exceptional performance as CEO, the ABC board has granted you an option to buy 10,000 shares of ABC stock at $100 per share. The option expires in five years. ABC stock is now selling at $80 per share. Even though you could, you won't exercise the option today because you would pay $100 for something that was only worth $80. However, within five years there is a good chance that ABC stock will trade well above $100 at some point, and when it does you will have the choice of exercising the option and making a profit. So you have a claim on a potential future profit, with the amount contingent on the future behavior of ABC stock price and contingent on when and if you decide to exercise your option. But today, neither you or ABC knows whether you will exercise the option.

---

*LIBOR stands for London Interbank Offered Rate.

Other forms of contingent claims are *intangible*, because the uncertain triggering events are not well defined. You went to the Harvard Business School hoping that it would improve your chances of building a successful, financially rewarding career. But Harvard did not contractually promise you such a result and you had no way of knowing exactly how or why it would happen, or even if it would. There would be a thousand contingencies along the way, few of which you could foresee. Nevertheless, on graduation day you were confident that you had earned the rights to something valuable, even though that value was intangible. Your Harvard degree is an intangible asset.

Corporations also have intangible claims of value, such as patent rights that have not yet been fully embodied into saleable products or royalty contracts. Sometimes a company's most valuable claim is the intangible value of its brand name and reputation, because they will produce profitable business opportunities in the future, many of which are not clearly identified today.

What You Owe Are Liabilities

"What You Owe," also called liabilities, is any and all claims that may obligate you to give up something of value now or in the future. Like assets, liabilities take myriad forms—often the mirror images of the assets we have just described. If I loan you money, I have an asset called a loan and you have the mirror image liability called a loan. What I own, you owe. So, like assets, liabilities can be fixed, variable, or contingent and some contingent liabilities can be intangible. If ABC has the threat of a professional liability suit being brought against it, it has an intangible liability, contingent on whether the suit is filed and how the case comes out. ABC may be required to pay out money in the future, but the timing, the amount, and the precise events leading to that outcome are ambiguous and highly uncertain. Nevertheless, the threat is real enough to keep you, the CEO, awake at night, even though the liability is intangible. It may also be real enough for investors to take $3 per share off of your stock price today.

What You Can Keep Is Your Net Worth

"What You Can Keep," or your net worth, is simply the value of "What You Own" (assets) minus the value of "What You Owe" (liabilities). Your net worth is what we really care about, not your assets or liabilities in isolation. If your net worth goes down, that is a bad outcome. If it goes up, that is a good outcome. If an event causes the value of your assets to go down, it may or may not be bad for you, depending on the effect the event had on the value of your liabilities. If the event caused the value of your liabilities to go down by more than it caused the value of your assets to go down, it was a good event for you because your net worth went up.

So in thinking about financial risk, we are focusing solely on the risk to your (or ABC's) net worth—

the chance that it could go down a given amount, in a given period of time, within a given probability (value at risk, VaR). In our examples, however, we look beneath VaR to see what is going on.

Because your net worth is the net result of what happens to the value of your assets and liabilities, we need to have a view of how your asset and liability values could change under various decisions and scenarios and assess the probabilities of those scenarios. That is the essence of financial risk management. Of course, since your assets and liabilities have complex and uncertain elements, determining their values can be quite daunting. This task is where accountants are supposed to be helpful, but they will almost always fall short of giving you a fair, accurate, and complete accounting of where you stand.

I have taken an expansive, comprehensive view of assets and liabilities that accountants would not put on a company's official books. Accountants believe that they are conservative folk and they don't like to put numbers on things that don't have notes or receipts or contracts attached. How would accountants handle the booking of ABC's threatened lawsuit, which I identified as an intangible liability? The accountants would politely ignore it in its early days. Later, they would allow it to appear as a vaguely worded footnote as the threat began to materialize. Finally, when reckoning day was unavoidable and soon, they would allow it to appear in the official liability accounts. Why do they wait so long to recognize reality? Accountants say that it would be hard to estimate a value for such a liability while the uncertainty and ambiguity is so high. True, but any reasonable estimate is likely to be more accurate than *zero*, which is the de facto number that they put on the liability by ignoring it.

Even worse, accountants can have a strange aversion to using current values, even when they are readily available. Banks, for example, have "investment" accounts and "trading" accounts. Accountants require, quite properly, that marketable securities in "trading" accounts be marked to market. If a bank bought a treasury bond for its trading account for $1,000 yesterday, and tomorrow's newspaper reports its current market price as $950, the bank must take a $50 loss per bond and carry the position on its official books at $950 per bond. So far, so good. But if the bank bought the *identical* bond yesterday for $1,000 per bond and put it into its *investment* account, the accountants would *not* require the bank to mark it to its readily determined current value of $950. It would remain on the books at $1,000 and the bank would *not* report a loss of $50 per bond. We have the plainly ludicrous result that the same bond is carried at two different values on the bank's books, depending only on the label of the file folder that holds it. How can this be? Good question. I have heard arguments that investment assets, unlike trading assets, are held for the long term and don't need to be sold now, therefore the loss (or gain) does not need to be taken yet. If you believe that a treasury bond is worth its original face value simply because you decided not to sell it today, then you will agree with the accountants. I don't.

Unfortunately, managers of banks have often been very eager to agree with them (unless of course, there were *gains* in the investment account; managers are practical people and are seldom bedeviled by foolish consistency). The tacit cooperation of the accountants has allowed some bank managers to obscure losses and hang on to large risk positions which, in some cases, endangered the solvency of their institutions.

Accountants also can have a strange aversion to using current values for *liabilities*, even though they may use current values for *identical* instruments booked as *assets*. Suppose ABC bank issued a long-term bond several years ago that was purchased, at $1,000 per bond, by a bond mutual fund. The bond trades on the market, and for whatever reason, has declined in value to $850 per bond today. You can look up the current value in the newspaper or on the internet. So can the accountants. When they do the books of the bond mutual fund, they see the ABC bond as an *asset* that must be valued at its current value of $850. So far, so good. But when they do the books of ABC bank, they see a *liability* that must be carried at its original value of $1,000 per bond. The *very same* instrument carried at different values, depending only on whether it appears in a liability file folder or an asset file folder. Why? Beats me. I am sure the accountants have their reasons, but they will have to write their own book.

These examples should be sufficient to convince you that you would be reckless to take the numbers of accountants at face value if you are trying to assess the real values and potential risks of a company's assets and liabilities.

Why have I gone out of my way to bash accountants, despite their good intentions, diligent work habits, and attention to detail? Because so-called conservative accountants can be quite dangerous. By ignoring realities that are evident to any sensible person having the same facts, accountants can (unintentionally) portray a healthy company as sick or a sick company as healthy. They can also create perverse incentives for managers to make poor decisions, because managers are often rewarded in the short run for what happens on the accounting books, even if the accounting does not reflect reality. What is conservative about that?

The point is this: Good risk managers *never, ever* take accounting numbers at face value. Accounting numbers can be useful input data, but without careful interpretation, they provide no *answers* that you can rely on to make good risk decisions. Good risk management is based on estimates of current and prospective values of assets and liabilities—*real* values. Real value can be traded for other things of real value, like a tank car full of oil, a 747, or the right to use the Disney logo on your toys. Accounting numbers may just be numbers. Your net worth is meaningless unless it can be used to buy you something that you want.

Because you are a good risk manager, you will focus on the current and prospective value of your net worth, determined as the net result of current and prospective changes in the values of your assets and liabilities. As CEO of ABC, you will develop a view of ABC's risk position by looking at *prospective changes in ABC's net worth under different scenarios and different decisions.*

A SIMPLE EXAMPLE: NOTES OR BONDS?

We start with a very simple example of how to assess the risk to a company's net worth. Pretend that ABC bank is a brand new company. Investors have just purchased $1 billion worth of newly issued ABC stock. The proceeds are sitting in your lower right-hand desk drawer, awaiting your decision on what to do with the money (Figure 7.1).

Note that the books balance. One billion dollars of assets minus $0 of liabilities equals $1.0 billion of net worth. The accountants would be proud of me, even after what I said about them earlier.

Now you must make your first decision as CEO. How are you going to invest the $1 billion? Pretend that only two investment choices are permitted by your board: (1) 2-year treasury notes, paying a fixed rate of interest of 4 percent; or (2) 30-year (non-callable) treasury bonds, paying a fixed rate of interest of 7 percent. Being an astute financier, you immediately realize that the bonds will give you

Figure 7.1
ABC's Balance Sheet on Day 1 (in millions of dollars)

Assets (What ABC Owns)	Liabilities (What ABC Owes)	Net Worth (What ABC Can Keep)
$1,000 Cash	$0	$1,000

more immediate income (at 7 percent) than the notes (at 4 percent). Bonds are looking good. But being an astute risk manager, you also realize that you need to understand the different risks of the two choices before you decide what to do.

Let's examine the potential risks of notes and bonds, using the risk types that we developed in Chapter 6.

Credit risk?   Notes: None

                     Bonds: None

Unless you believe that the U.S. government can default, you are certain to get back your $1 billion and to receive all of your promised interest payments on schedule.

Currency risk?   Notes: None

                     Bonds: None

Notes and bonds are both denominated in U.S. dollars, so there is no risk that changes in currency rates will affect the amount of dollars that you will receive in the future. [We assume that you measure your wealth in U.S. dollars, not francs (excuse me, euros). Readers living in France may be uncomfortable with this assumption. But this opens up a long and confusing discussion that we will ignore.]

Liquidity risk?   Notes: Negligible

                     Bonds: Negligible

No asset is perfectly liquid and bonds are slightly less liquid than notes. But both are so liquid that it is highly likely that you will be able to sell either notes or bonds quickly at a fair market price. We are comfortable ignoring this risk in this example. But this may not always be wise, particularly if you find yourself owning a large fraction of a particular bond issue, as might be the case if you were a bond dealer or hedge fund.

Commodity risk?   Notes: None

Bonds: None

Both notes and bonds pay out in dollars, not pork bellies.

Equity risk?   Notes: None

Bonds: None

Neither notes nor bonds give you an ownership interest in the U.S. government (you already have that as a voter and taxpayer). You get paid a fixed amount, regardless of whether the government makes a profit.

Operating risk?   Notes: Negligible

Bonds: Negligible

There is a slight chance that a clerical error, a computer problem, or some other snafu might delay your payments. This delay doesn't happen very often with government securities and when it does, the guilty party almost always covers any losses.

Interest rate risk?   Notes: Very low

Bonds: Very high

Here we come to the only significant difference in risk between notes and bonds—interest rate risk. Notes have a very short maturity compared to bonds (2 years versus 30 years). Therefore, changes in interest rates change the value of notes much less than bonds (see discussion in Chapter 6 of interest rate risk). But we need to quantify this difference before you make your investment decision.

Figure 7.2 summarizes our risk analysis so far. We know that bonds offer higher current income than notes (7 percent versus 4 percent) but have higher interest rate risk, but how much higher? Using standard bond math we can compute by how

Figure 7.2
Risk Characteristics

Risk Type	Notes	Bonds
Credit	None	None
Currency	None	None
Liquidity	Negligible	Negligible
Commodity	None	None
Equity	None	None
Operating	Negligible	Negligible
Interest Rate	Very low	Very high

Figure 7.3
Interest Rate Risk of Notes and Bonds

Market Interest Rate (%)	Market Price		
	Note (1-Year) 4% Coupon	Note (2-Year) 4% Coupon	Bond (30-Year) 7% Coupon
1	102.97	105.91	254.85
2	101.96	103.88	211.98
3	100.97	101.91	178.40
4	100.00	100.00	151.88
5	99.05	98.14	130.74
6	98.11	96.33	113.76
7	97.20	94.58	100.00
8	96.30	92.87	88.74
9	95.41	91.20	79.45
10	94.55	89.59	71.72
11	93.69	88.01	65.22
12	92.86	86.48	59.72

much a given change in interest rates changes the values of notes and bonds. The results are given in Figure 7.3.

Now, Figure 7.4 shows the same information expressed as *changes*: Note that the sensitivity of note and bond prices to changes in market interest rates increases with maturity. For a 2 percent increase in rates, the 1-year note loses $1.89 in value, the 2-year note loses $3.67 and the 30-year bond loses $20.55. A given change in market interest rates has a much

Figure 7.4
Changes in Market Interest Rate and Price

Change in Market Interest Rate (%)	Change in Market Price		
	Note (1-Year) 4% Coupon	Note (2-Year) 4% Coupon	Bond (30-Year) 7% Coupon
−5	—	—	+111.98
−4	+4.00	+8.00	+78.40
−3	+2.97	+5.91	+51.88
−2	+1.96	+3.88	+30.74
−1	+0.97	+1.91	+13.76
0	0	0	0
+1	−0.95	−1.86	−11.26
+2	−1.89	−3.67	−20.55
+3	−2.80	−5.42	−28.28
+4	−3.70	−7.13	−34.78
+5	−4.59	−8.80	−40.28
+6	−5.45	−10.41	−44.97
+7	−6.31	−11.99	−49.02
+8	−7.14	−13.52	−52.53

greater effect on the long-term bond than on the short-term notes. In an environment of volatile interest rates, long-term bond prices are very volatile and therefore are much riskier to hold than short-term notes.

The next step is to develop your views on the likely future volatility of interest rates, so you can assess the likely volatility of ABC's net worth under different investment strategies. Unfortunately, if you are like me, you don't have any views on this subject at the moment, so you call in your high-priced economists and bond traders to help.

After you offer them each a cigar from your walk-in humidor, you ask them what they think about the future volatility of interest rates. Like most experts, they answer a question with a question: "What interest rates?" You say, "Short-term notes and long-term bonds." They ask, "Over what time period?" Knowing that your next bonus will be based on the state of the bank one year from today, you say, "Over the next year." The economist gives a five-minute discourse on the likely mood swings of Alan Greenspan. You turn to the bond trader, who gives a five-minute discourse on the likely mood swings of George Soros, the famous investor who can move markets. He also glances at his watch because while he is up here in the boardroom shooting the breeze with you, he is not down on the trading floor making money.

You say to them both, "That's all very interesting, but you are not answering my question. Let me be very specific. I want you to give me three scenarios each for notes and for bonds: the expected scenario, where there is a equal chance of rates being above it or below it; the high-rate scenario, where there is only a 1 percent chance that rates will be above it; and the low-rate scenario, where there is only a 1 percent chance that rates will be below it. All numbers are as of one year from today."

They are both very uncomfortable committing themselves to views expressed in this form. The economist wants to say "On the other hand. . . ." The trader wants to say, "Just do it." So, it takes you a while to wring answers out of them. Of course, they each have a different view. So you have to take it from there. You take what they gave you, combine it with your own hunches and your own judgments of the biases of the economist and of the trader and come up with *your* view of how interest rates might change over the coming year. How do you do this? Don't ask me; that is one of the things that CEOs are paid to do. You take out your gold Cross pen and write out a table on your yellow pad that looks like Figure 7.5.

Some people might complain that your views are a bit coarse. Isn't there a chance that note rates could be 2.5 percent or 9 percent? Or that bond rates could be 3 percent or 13 percent? Of course there is, but while you are busy assigning probability numbers to 37 different possible rate outcomes, the bond market may be moving away from you or you may miss your board meeting at 3 o'clock. In fact, you have done more than most VaR experts, who would only have bothered to come up with the 1 percent high-rate scenario (and they would have tied up your main-

Figure 7.5
CEO's Interest Rate Views

Scenario	Probability (%)	End of Year Note Rate (%)	End of Year Bond Rate (%)
Low Rates	1	2	4
Expected Rates	98	3	7
High Rates	1	11	12

frame for five hours to do the calculations). In any event, these are the views you are willing to bet your career on, you are the CEO, end of story.

Now we must see how ABC's net worth would be affected by different investment decisions under each of your interest rate scenarios. Remember, your board has restricted you to one of only two investment strategies. Invest the $1 billion of net worth in 2-year notes or invest it all in bonds. Apparently you did not choose your board for their imagination or flexibility. Perhaps you had some takeover defense in mind.

Let's run through the expected rate scenario, assuming we invested in 2-year notes.

- Today, we invest in $1.000 billion worth of 2-year notes paying 4 percent.
- Over the next year, we earn $1.000 billion × .04 = $40 million of interest.
- One year from today, market rates on notes have changed from 4 percent to 3 percent (according to your expected rate scenario). We have $1.000 billion on notes still on the books with a one-year remaining maturity. We need to mark those notes to market so that our assets are shown at fair value. A 1-year, 4 percent coupon note is now worth $100.97, so ABC's note position is worth $1.0097 billion.
- So, one year from today, ABC's assets will be: $1.0097 billion in notes plus $40 million in cash = $1.0497 billion.
- Since ABC has no liabilities, ABC's net worth is also $1.0497 billion.

- ABC's income will be $40 million (interest earnings) plus $9.7 million (the increase in value of the notes) = $49.7 million. Note that ABC's income equals its change in net worth (1,049.7 − 1,000 = 49.7).

Now we run through the expected rate scenario assuming we invested in 30-year bonds.

- Today, we invest in $1.000 billion worth of 30-year bonds paying 7 percent.
- Over the next year, we earn $1.000 billion × .07 = $70 million of interest.
- One year from today, market rates on bonds are unchanged at 7 percent (according to your expected rate scenario). We have $1.000 billion of bonds still on the books with a 29-year remaining maturity. We need to mark those bonds to market so that our assets are shown at fair value. A 29-year, 7 percent coupon bond is worth $100 when market rates are 7 percent, so ABC's bond position is still worth $1.000 billion.
- So, one year from today, ABC's assets will be: $1.000 billion in 30-year bonds plus $70 million in cash = $1.070 billion.
- Since ABC has zero liabilities, ABC's net worth is also = $1.070 billion.
- ABC's income will be: $70 million (interest earnings) plus $0 million (no change in value of the bonds) = $70 million. Note that ABC's income equals its change in net worth (1,070 − 1,000 = 70).

So if the expected rate scenario prevails, ABC will earn $49.7 million if you invest in notes and $70.0 million if you invest in bonds. Those bonds are tempting. But wait, you need to look at the other scenarios before you decide.

Now we go through the same calculations for the low rate scenario and for the high rate scenario and summarize our analysis in Figure 7.6.

Because we have defined "risk" as the volatility of ABC's net worth, the bond strategy is clearly riskier than the note strategy. If you invest in notes, the range of possible outcomes is –$23.1 million to +$59.6 million. But if you invest in bonds, the range of possible outcomes is –$331.1 to +$579.5.

Figure 7.6
Decision Tree for Investing in Notes or Bonds

STRATEGY	PROBABILITY	SCENARIO FOR RATES	CHANGE IN NET WORTH ($ millions)
	1%	Low	+59.6
Invest in notes	98%	Expected	+49.7
	1%	High	–23.1
	1%	Low	+579.5
Invest in bonds	98%	Expected	+70.0
	1%	High	–331.1

The analysis is done. What are you going to do? Bonds are very tempting because, according to *your* beliefs about future interest rates, there is a 99 percent chance that the bond investment will be more profitable than the note investment and will include a shot at a bonanza of $579.5 million. There is, however, a 1 percent chance that ABC will lose $331 million and that you will lose your job as CEO. Notes are much safer but do not offer much profit potential. You are very comfortable that the risk is worth the reward so you decide to invest in the bonds.

EXAMPLE 2: APPLY SOME LEVERAGE

In fact, you are so comfortable with your chosen investment strategy that you want to invest even more. But you need more money. Every dime of shareholder funds has already been committed to the bond investment. Fortunately, ABC is a large bank. You know that you can easily raise another billion dollars by issuing one-year certificates of deposit (CDs) at 4.5 percent. That would allow you to buy $2 billion of bonds rather than just $1 billion. You have entered the wonderful world of leverage.

So we redo our risk analysis accordingly. As an example, take the low rate scenario assuming a bond investment strategy:

- Today, we borrow $1.000 billion by issuing 1-year CDs at a fixed interest rate of 4.5 percent.

- We invest in $2.000 billion of 30-year bonds paying 7 percent, using $1,000 million of shareholder funds and the $1.000 billion proceeds from issuing the CD.
- Over the next year, we earn $2.000 billion × .07 = $140 million of interest income from the bonds. We pay $1.000 billion × .045 = $45 million of interest expense on the CDs. So our net interest income is $140 million–$45 million = $95 million.
- One year from today, market rates on bonds have fallen to 4 percent (according to your low rate scenario). We have $2.000 billion of bonds still on the books with a 29-year remaining maturity. We need to mark those bonds to market so that our assets are shown at fair value. A 29-year, 7 percent coupon bond is worth $150.95 when market rates are 4 percent, so ABC's bond position is worth $2.000 billion × 1.5095 = $3.019 billion.
- So, one year from today, ABC's assets will be: $3.019 billion in 30-year bonds plus $95 million in cash from net interest income = $3.114 billion.
- Since ABC has $1.000 billion in liabilities (the CD), ABC's net worth is $3.114 billion–$1.000 billion = $2.114 billion.
- ABC's income will be $95 million (net interest earnings) plus $1.019 billion (the increase in value of the bonds) = $1.114 billion. Note that ABC's income equals its change in net worth: $2.114 billion–$1.000 billion = $1.114 billion.

Under the low rate scenario, a leveraged investment in bonds produces a profit of over a billion dollars, more than doubling shareholder net worth in just one year! Without the leverage, the profit under that scenario would have been only $579.5 million. Time to buy that new ocean-going yacht that you have had your eye on. That's the power of leverage in action.

But, of course, life is not that easy. As the old saying goes, "Leverage works both ways." Just look at what happens under the high rate scenario:

- Today, we borrow $1.000 billion by issuing one-year CDs at a fixed interest rate of 4.5 percent.
- We invest in $2.000 billion of 30-year bonds paying 7 percent, using $1.000 billion of shareholder funds and the $1.000 billion proceeds from issuing the CD.
- Over the next year, we earn $2.000 billion × .07 = $140 million of interest income from the bonds. We pay $1.000 billion × .045 = $45 million of interest expense on the CDs. So our net interest income is $140 million – $45 million = $95 million.
- One year from today, market rates on bonds have risen to 12 percent (according to your high rate scenario). We have $2.000 billion of bonds still on the books with a 29-year remaining maturity. We need to mark those bonds to market so that our assets are shown at fair value. A 29-year, 7 percent coupon bond is worth $59.89 when market rates are 12 percent, so ABC's bond position is worth $2.000 billion × .5989 = $1.1978 billion.

- So, one year from today, ABC's assets will be $1.1978 billion in 30-year bonds plus $95 million in cash from net interest income = $1.2928 billion.
- Since ABC has $1.000 billion in liabilities (the CD), ABC's net worth is $1.2928 billion − $1.000 billion = $292.8 million.
- ABC's *net loss* will be $95 million (net interest earnings) minus $802.2 million (the decrease in value of the bonds) = $707.2 million. Note that ABC's net loss equals its change in net worth: $292.8 million − $1.000 billion = −$707.2 million.

Figure 7.7 summarizes our decision tree.

Figure 7.7
Leverage or No Leverage with Bond Investment

STRATEGY	PROBABILITY	SCENARIO FOR RATES	CHANGE IN NET WORTH ($ millions)
	1%	Low	+579.5
No leverage	98%	Expected	+70.0
	1%	High	−331.1
	1%	Low	+1114.0
Leverage	98%	Expected	+95.0
	1%	High	−707.2

Well, the high rate scenario isn't much fun at all. Leverage magnified the loss from $331.1 million to $707.2 million and the shareholders' net worth declined from $1.000 billion to $292.8 million for a loss of 71 percent for the year. You are going to be reading unflattering stories about yourself in the right-hand column of page one of the *Wall Street Journal*. Of course, you believe that there is only a 1 percent chance of this disaster unfolding, so you forge ahead with your decision to make a leveraged investment in bonds.

EXAMPLE 3: EURO K, I'M OK

Now you are really pumped up about making big money in the financial markets. You think you have made a savvy bet on interest rates, but why stop there? Last Saturday your caddy at the country club made some very incisive comments on the euro and you both concluded that it had to strengthen against the dollar over the next year, from its current value of 1.1 euros per dollar. At the nineteenth hole, you and your caddy came up with the forecast shown in Figure 7.8.

This forecast is just too good to pass up. You decide to bet on the euro by borrowing $1.000 billion dollars for one year at 4.5 percent to invest in one-year euro notes issued by the German government, paying 5 percent in euros. Like U.S. government obligations, these short-term German government obligations carry no credit risk, equity risk, or commodity risk. They carry negligible liquidity and

Figure 7.8
Forecast for the Euro

Scenario	Probability (%)	Value of Euro at Year-End (euros/$)
Euro Strengthens	70	0.90
Euro Holds Steady	29	1.10
Euro Collapses	1	1.50

operating risks. They carry a small interest rate risk, which you will hedge away by funding them with borrowings of the same maturity. From ABC's point of view, as a U.S. institution, the euro notes carry only currency risk. Under your euro strengthens scenario, the following list shows what would happen:

- You issue $1.000 billion of ABC 1-year CDs at 4.5 percent.
- You exchange the $1.000 billion for E1.100 billion and use the euros to buy E1.100 billion of the euro notes at today's exchange rate of 1.1 euro/$.
- Over the next year, you will earn E1.100 billion × .05 = E55 million in interest income. Under the euro strengthens scenario you will exchange the euros for dollars at .9 euro/$, and receive E55 million/.9 = $61.1 million. You will pay $1.000 billion × .045 = $45 million in interest expense on the ABC CD. So your net interest income *in dollars* = $61.1 – $45= $16.1 million.
- At the end of one year, the euro note will mature and pay you E1.100 billion, which you will

exchange for E1.100/.9 = $1.2222 billion. Your ABC CD will mature and you will pay out $1.000 billion.
- The net gain from this transaction is $16.1 million of net interest income + ($1.2222 – $1.000) billion of currency gain = $238.3 million.

Not bad. Especially since you used other peoples' money to finance the whole bet. Leverage is fantastic (if you are right). Of course if you were very wrong and the euro collapses scenario comes true, you won't be very happy:

- You issue $1.000 billion of ABC 1-year CDs at 4.5 percent.
- You exchange the $1.000 billion for E1.100 billion and use the euros to buy E1.100 billion of the euro note at today's exchange rate of 1.1 euro/$.
- Over the next year, you will earn E1.100 billion × .05 = E55 million in interest income. Under the euro collapses scenario you will exchange the euros for dollars at 1.5 euro/$, and receive E55 million/1.5 = $36.7 million. You will pay $1.000 billion × .045 = $45 million in interest expense on the ABC CD. So your net interest income *in dollars* = $36.7 – $45 = –$8.3 million. Oops, not so good.
- At the end of one year, the euro note will mature and pay you E1.100 billion, which you will exchange for E1.100/1.5 = $733.3. Your ABC CD will mature and you will pay out $1.000 billion. Not very good at all. You have

come up short by $733.3 - $1000 = -$266.7 million.

- The net loss from this transaction is -$8.3 million of net interest income - $266.7 of currency loss = -$275 million.

Losing $275 million will not endear you to the compensation committee of the board, so you had better be right. But you are confident that you are right because you assigned only a 1 percent chance that the euro could collapse over the next year. We complete the analysis by doing the same calculations for the euro holds steady scenario and summarize as shown in Figure 7.9.

Figure 7.9
Consequences of the Bet on the Euro

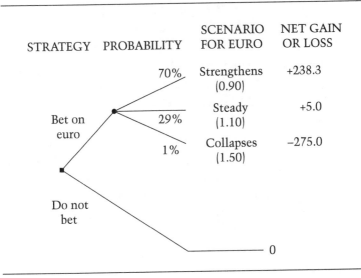

STRATEGY	PROBABILITY	SCENARIO FOR EURO	NET GAIN OR LOSS
	70%	Strengthens (0.90)	+238.3
Bet on euro	29%	Steady (1.10)	+5.0
	1%	Collapses (1.50)	-275.0
Do not bet			0

Figure 7.10
ABC's Balance Sheet Today

Assets	Liabilities	Net Worth
$2,000 Bonds	$1,000 1-year CDs	
1,000 Euro Notes	1,000 1-year CDs	
$3,000 Total	$2,000 Total	$1,000

So now you have three bets going: the bond bet, the euro bet, and the leverage bet. We need to see how all of these *together* might affect the ABC shareholder net worth.

Today, after you placed your bets, the balance sheet of ABC looks like that shown in Figure 7.10. One year from today, the state of ABC's balance sheet will depend on how the scenarios played out. Figure 7.11 shows the possible events that could occur (according to your beliefs).

Why didn't you fill in the probabilities for each combination of outcomes for the interest rate bet and the euro bet? You previously assigned probabilities to each scenario separately. Isn't this enough? No. Because what you need, for example, is the probability that low rates *and* euro strengthens *will both happen*. You haven't expressed a view on that yet. You assigned a 1 percent probability to low rates and a 70 percent chance to euro strengthens, but you need to assess how the two scenarios are *correlated* with each other (Chapter 2) before you can say how likely it is that low rates and euro strengthens *will occur together*.

Figure 7.11
Possible Events

Outcome for Interest Rate Bet	Outcome for Euro Bet	Combined Probability
Low Rates	Strengthens	?
	Holds steady	?
	Collapses	?
Expected Rates	Strengthens	?
	Holds steady	?
	Collapses	?
High Rates	Strengthens	?
	Holds steady	?
	Collapses	?

You consider calling in your economist, your bond trader, and your caddy to get their views but you are already running late for your board meeting and they will just disagree with each other anyway.

At first, you draw a complete blank—you don't have the foggiest idea about the connection, if any, between U.S. interest rates and Eurocurrency rates. You know that there is probably some economic relationship between the two but you can't think of what it might be. Economics 101 at Harvard was a long time ago. Does this mean that you cannot assign probabilities to the combined outcomes of the scenarios and therefore cannot complete your risk analysis? Certainly not. You are a risk manager *who has to make a decision right now*, not a scientist writing a journal article who can ponder the question for a few months. If you cannot imagine how or whether the occurrence of low rates might affect the probability that euro strengthens will occur, then you must act as if you believe that they are *independent of each other* and therefore *uncorrelated* with each other. In your state of pure ignorance, the occurrence of low rates (or expected rates or high rates) does not give you any information about whether euro strengthens (or euro holds or euro collapses) has occurred. Or vice versa.

If you believe that the rate scenarios and the euro scenarios are independent of each other, then your probability assessments are as shown in Figure 7.12.

Figure 7.12
Combined Probabilities If Rates and Euros Are Independent

Outcome for Interest Rate Bet (probability in percentage)	Outcome for Euro Bet (probability in percentage)		Combined Probability
Low Rates (1)	Strengthens	(70)	.01 × .70 = .0070
	Holds Steady	(29)	.01 × .29 = .0029
	Collapses	(1)	.01 × .01 = .0001
Expected Rates (98)	Strengthens	(70)	.98 × .70 = .6860
	Holds Steady	(29)	.98 × .29 = .2842
	Collapses	(1)	.98 × .01 = .0098
High Rates (1)	Strengthens	(70)	.01 × .70 = .0070
	Holds Steady	(29)	.01 × .29 = .0029
	Collapses	(1)	.01 × .01 = .0001
			1.000

Because you believe in independence, the probabilities for the euro scenarios are the same in all interest rate scenarios.

Now we are ready to see what happens to ABC shareholder net worth under all the combined scenarios. For each combination (say low rates and euro strengthens) we calculate the financial results for ABC, just as we did in the foregoing examples. The results are summarized in Figure 7.13.

Under your financial strategy (bonds plus euros plus leverage) and given your beliefs about the

Figure 7.13
Effect on ABC's Net Worth
Bonds + Euros + Leverage

Outcome for Interest Rates	Outcome for Euro	Probability	ABC's Change in Net Worth	ABC's End of Year Net Worth
Low Rates	Strengthens	.0070	+1352.3	2352.3
	Holds Steady	.0029	+1119.0	2119.0
	Collapses	.0001	+839.0	1839.0
Expected Rates	Strengthens	.6860	+333.3	1333.3
	Holds Steady	.2842	+100.0	1100.0
	Collapses	.0098	−180.0	820.0
High Rates	Strengthens	.0070	−468.9	531.1
	Holds Steady	.0029	−702.2	297.8
	Collapses	.0001	−982.2	17.8
		1.000		

future, there is only a 1 percent chance that ABC could lose more than $180 million (.007 + .0029 + .0001). A VaR expert would say that ABC's VaR is $180 million. And that's probably all he would say because some VaR people equate "VaR" with "risk" and leave it at that. But you can see that there is a lot more to the story:

- There is one chance in 1,000 of wiping out nearly all of ABC's net worth by losing $982.2 million. A financial catastrophe for ABC and a career-ender for you. Highly improbable, according to *you*, but a possibility that should not be ignored.
- There is a 98 percent chance that ABC will make money (.0079 + .0029 + .0001 + .6860 + .2842). Life should always be this easy.
- There is a .99 percent chance of making more than $1 billion (.0070 + .0029). A nice lottery ticket for ABC shareholders and a shot at glory for you.

This risk analysis gives you a warm glow as prospects look very good for ABC and for you, with only the tiniest probability of a real disaster. But now you begin to feel a bit queasy as you begin to wonder about your stated belief that U.S. interest rates and Eurocurrency rates were independent of each other and thus uncorrelated. You remember that the capital markets are global, with investors switching in and out of bonds, currencies, stocks, commodities, and other tradable assets in search of the best returns. If so, changes in market interest rates of U.S. bonds probably affect Eurocurrency rates, or vice versa, as investors buy and sell euro- and dollar-denominated assets against each other. As you think about this, your beliefs begin to change. You now believe that a high rate scenario would imply a much higher probability of a collapse of Eurocurrency rates as investors chased the higher-yielding dollar assets. Likewise, you now believe that a low rate scenario would imply a much lower probability of a collapse of Eurocurrency rates. These kinds of thoughts roll around your mind, changing your beliefs about the connections among the possible outcomes. Using your CEO intuition and judgment, you come to your new probability beliefs shown in Figure 7.14.

You didn't change your euro forecast under the expected rate scenario. But under the high rate scenario you substantially increased the odds of euro collapse and of euro holds steady. Similarly, under the low rate scenario, you increased the odds of euro strengthens and reduced the odds of euro holding steady. Do these assessments make sense? You could ask your economist and I could ask mine, but would they agree? In any case, time is up, you have to decide what to do, and these are your revised beliefs. You have to act on them. Figure 7.15 shows where ABC stands now.

There is still only a 1 percent chance that ABC could lose more than $180 million (.0030 + .0050 + .0020). So, your change of beliefs did not happen to change your VaR. Your VaR expert would give you

Figure 7.14
Revised Beliefs: Combined Probabilities If Rates
and Euros Are Related

Outcome for Interest Rate Bet (Probability in percentage)	Outcome for Euro Bet (Probability in percentage)		Combined Probability
Low Rates	Strengthens	(90)	.01 × .90 = .0090
(1)	Holds Steady	(9)	.01 × .09 = .0009
	Collapses	(1)	.01 × .01 = .0001
Expected Rates	Strengthens	(70)	.98 × .70 = .6860
(98)	Holds Steady	(29)	.98 × .29 = .2842
	Collapses	(1)	.98 × .01 = .0098
High Rates	Strengthens	(30)	.01 × .30 = .0030
(1)	Holds Steady	(50)	.01 × .50 = .0050
	Collapses	(20)	.01 × .20 = .0020
			1.000

the same risk assessment that he gave you before. This doesn't seem right does it? Once again, there is more to the story:

- There is now a 20 out of 1,000 chance of wiping out nearly all of ABC's net worth by losing $982.2 million, compared to the 1 out of 1,000 chance under your old beliefs. The probability of disaster is now 20 times higher than it was under your old beliefs. Although it is still low, the prospect of disaster becomes harder to ignore.

Figure 7.15
Effect on ABC's Net Worth under Revised Beliefs

Outcome for Interest Rates	Outcome for Euro	Probability	ABC's Change in Net Worth	ABC's End of Year Net Worth
Low Rates	Strengthens	.0090	+1352.3	2352.3
	Holds steady	.0009	+1119.0	2119.0
	Collapses	.0001	+839.0	1839.0
Expected Rates	Strengthens	.6860	+333.3	1333.3
	Holds steady	.2842	+100.0	1100.0
	Collapses	.0098	−180.0	820.0
High Rates	Strengthens	.0030	−468.9	531.1
	Holds steady	.0050	−702.2	297.8
	Collapses	.0020	−982.2	17.8
		1.0000		

Even with your revised beliefs, the potential rewards seem attractive relative to the risks. So you go ahead with your strategies of levering up, investing in bonds, and making a currency bet on the euro.

After going through all this analysis, are we sure that you made the best possible decisions? No.

First, you never assessed anyone's utility function for changes in ABC's net worth, so you don't know exactly what preferences you are trying to serve. But who do you ask? ABC? ABC is a corporation, not a person. ABC's shareholders? They are the legal owners of ABC and are the rightful beneficiaries (or victims) of changes in ABC's net worth, so you know that you should be trying to do the best that you can for them. But there are so many shareholders, and to make things even more difficult, many of them are institutions like mutual funds. Do mutual funds have the same interests and preferences as human shareholders? Even the human shareholders are likely to differ among themselves when it comes to preferences for risk and return. What do you do? Just because the risk/return analysis feels good to you, the CEO of ABC, doesn't necessarily mean that you are making a good risk and return tradeoff on behalf of ABC's shareholders.

There is a camp of financial theorists that says that managers of corporations should ignore all risks that investors can manage better for themselves by adjusting the mix of their individual portfolios. In our example, ABC shareholders who like your bond bet but don't like your euro bet could undo the euro bet in their own portfolios by buying the stock of a bank that was taking the opposite view. Or the dissenting investors could even take the opposite currency bet themselves, leaving them with ABC stock minus ABC's currency bet.

This point is, in principle, a very good one. Don't waste your time or ABC's resources managing risks that ABC's shareholders can manage better for themselves in their own portfolios. But exactly what are those risks in reality? How do the dissenting investors know what currency bet that you, the CEO of ABC, are about to take? Even if they know, do they have the time or the ability to undo it in their own portfolios? They do not all have the same access to the financial markets that a large global bank like

ABC enjoys. ABC can transact at favorable rates not available to most investors. What if ABC takes large risks and goes bankrupt? Can ABC shareholders really protect themselves against the contingent costs of the bankruptcy process or the losses caused by dissipating the valuable human capital embodied in ABC's organization? Can ABC shareholders simply rely on the luck of naïve diversification in their own portfolios to make everything come out all right in the end? We could debate for a very long time and still not come up with a clear and simple rule for you to follow.

As a practical matter, we know that exposing ABC shareholders to potential reductions in ABC's net worth, unaccompanied by attractive opportunities for *increases* in ABC's net worth, is very unlikely to be a good thing for your career as CEO. So doing a risk analysis that weighs unfavorable volatility in ABC's net worth against potential gains in ABC's net worth is reasonable. Your most important job as CEO is to assess the preferences of your shareholder constituencies as best you can and act accordingly. This task is difficult, but that is another reason why you get paid the big bucks. ABC shareholders will vote with their feet in any case, so over time you will end up with the shareholders you deserve. And they will end up with the CEO they deserve, which may or may not be you.

The murky and conflicting nature of shareholder preferences is not the most important reason why we cannot be sure that you made the best possible risk decision. There were many, many alternatives for acting on your beliefs about interest rates and currency rates that you did not identify or consider (or rather, *your board of directors* did not allow you to consider). To bet on falling rates, you could have used interest rate futures, interest rate swaps, interest rate options, and other types of bonds of various maturities. Some stocks might also be used as part of an interest rate bet. Likewise, there were scores of ways to bet on your belief that the euro would strengthen. Some of these alternatives may have offered better rewards at the same risk or the same reward at lower risks. A crucial part of good risk management is identifying and comparing a wide range of opportunities to see what offers the best returns for the risks taken.

We also neglected other kinds of risks a bank typically takes. A large global financial institution is engaged in businesses that create an incredibly complex portfolio of risks and opportunities. The bank lends money to thousands of borrowers under many different credit structures. Its trading rooms around the world take currency positions in several major and minor currencies in many different instruments and buy and sell sovereign bonds, corporate bonds and loans, commodities, and equities. The bank enters into options, futures, and derivatives contracts that embody nearly every risk type and tenor imaginable in order to acquire desired risks and shed undesired risks. Its investment banking arm offers to underwrite new issues of equities and bonds for corporations and governments issuers around the world, taking some risk that the market will not buy the entire issue at the price guaranteed to the issuer. The bank offers mergers and acquisition services and other strategic advice to corporations for a fee and by doing so takes a risk that its advice turns out badly and the client sues. Its investment management arm manages mutual funds and other investment accounts for others and takes a risk that it may breach its investment guidelines and be required to refund the losses it caused in client portfolios. The bank offers a myriad of transaction processing services that might create operating errors that must be fixed at great expense. Its insurance arm may misjudge the risks of the Atlantic hurricane season and suffer large underwriting losses. Its credit card division might be hit with millions in uncollectable debt if a serious recession unfolds. With thousands of customers and thousands of different types of transactions created in far-flung locations, the number of possible permutations in risk positions is mind-boggling.

At first blush, it might seem impossible for the management of a large, global financial institution to know what is going on, let alone control it. But modern risk management techniques, together with other good management practices, can give managers enough knowledge and control to reduce the chance of a serious accident to acceptable levels and to allow attractive businesses to be pursued responsibly. To a large degree, financial institutions can now choose which risks they will take and which they will not.

The first step to gaining control over a volatile environment is for the firm to commit itself to good risk management. This commitment is not easy for it demands attention, resources, and the willingness, if necessary, to fundamentally change the way the firm is managed. Many people resist such a painful process. Even today, many firms have not made a full commitment. Ironically, half measures can be more dangerous than no measures, for a firm may become dangerously aggressive if it believes, erroneously, that its risks are under control. Because of the pain, difficulty, and expense, no firm can be truly committed to good risk management without the active and enthusiastic leadership of the CEO and board of directors. This statement was doubly true in the early days when modern risk management was not yet recognized as a necessary practice by regulators and investors. The courage and foresight of the pioneers, like Charlie Sanford of Bankers Trust, is truly remarkable. Bankers Trust was the first bank to install a comprehensive enterprise risk management system (called RAROC, for "Risk Adjusted Return on Capital"). Aided by RAROC, Bankers Trust produced an unbroken record of strong trading profits that lasted for many years. RAROC also contributed to Bankers Trust's early leadership in innovative risk management products and in the development of the market for the sale of commercial loans.

The next step is to adopt a consistent framework for defining, identifying, and quantifying all types of risk that can arise in all the businesses of the firm. This framework allows all risks to be compared fairly to each other, to be weighed against each other, and to be aggregated into a consolidated view of the firm's entire risk exposure. It also reduces the chance that an important risk will go unrecognized. Fortunately, such frameworks now exist for any financial firm to use, thanks to the pioneers who developed them.

The next step is to gather the data on businesses and transactions that are necessary to feed the analytical framework. This process is very difficult and expensive. In a large financial firm, risk management data systems cost millions of dollars to install and maintain, but it is vitally necessary. Faulty data can give disastrously wrong signals. Fortunately, complete, fine-grained detail is not usually necessary. Good risk managers can make intelligent approximations that save money without sacrificing essential kernels of risk information.

With the analytical framework and data in place, the firm has good risk information available. This compilation is a giant step, but then comes the hard part. Good risk information has no value to the firm if the people who actually make the business decisions never use it. Risk management is about making better decisions, not about discovering interesting truths for their own sake.

Why wouldn't decision makers use information so important to the organization? There are many reasons. They may not understand it because it is expressed in unfamiliar language. They may not be eager to have their activities subjected to a new form of scrutiny and control (remember the extreme example of the rogue trader). They may be reluctant to abandon comfortable habits and easy rules of thumb that no longer can be defended, now that a better way to make decisions has arrived. They may fear that they will become obsolete because they cannot adapt to a new way of doing business.

Or, in their defense, the decision makers may know that the risk information does not describe the realities of their business accurately and to act on it uncritically would lead to bad decisions for the company. People who live inside a business every day know things about it that an outside observer does not know. These gritty business realities must be confronted and incorporated into the risk information. Involving decision makers in the design and continual testing of a risk management system not only makes it more realistic, it gives decision makers a stake in the system that increases their ability and willingness to use the system in their business decisions. Risk management systems that are imposed on decision makers without their genuine involvement are likely to fail from lack of use or lack of realism.

Now the firm has risk information that decision makers are willing to admit is relevant and useful and that will continually be improved through constant give and take between risk experts and decision makers. What else must management do? The firm must make it absolutely clear that it wants actual business decisions to be made in a way that reflects the risks being taken. Over time, a business must earn a return that compensates the firm for the risks inherent in the business or the business will be restructured or shut down. The performance of individual decision makers is judged in the same way. Promotions and compensation are linked to risk-adjusted results. When making proposals to top management, decision makers are expected to articulate clearly the nature and the amount of risks involved, to describe how they will manage those risks and to justify the risks by the potential rewards. High profits, by themselves, are not enough if excessive risks are taken. Losses taken through ignorance of risk will not be forgiven lightly.

Just as important, top management must take the same medicine that it prescribes for the rest of the organization. There is nothing more convincing than leading by example. Top management must be seen to make its decisions using the risk framework and discipline that it expects others to use. When it justifies its actions to the organization, it must include a credible view of the risks involved and what senior management is doing to manage those risks. In particular, it must be seen to be managing the company with a coherent view of the company's entire portfolio of risks. *And it will actually have that view* if it committed itself to a good risk management culture and carried through on that commitment.

Building a strong risk management culture is not for the faint-hearted or fuzzy-brained. It takes vision, courage, discipline, and very hard work. Because many firms fall short, it can be a powerful competitive advantage for those companies that succeed. Even though no company, however good, lives up to the ideal, the effort to do so makes the company stronger and smarter.

As you see, our simple examples barely scratched the surface of the complexities involved in properly managing the risks of a major financial institution, but now you may have a new appreciation of how it should be done. The better-managed banks of the world go through a process much like we did, only much more complex because of the vast range of their activities. These banks have a reasoned portfolio view of the risks that they are taking and how their shareholders' financial welfare could be affected by the volatility of the business environment in which they operate. They make decisions every day to adjust this risk profile to try to improve the balance of risk and return facing their institutions.

This is not to say that they have explicitly identified every contingency and evaluated all of their possible outcomes. Doing so is still impossible, even with hundreds of experts and enormous computing power. Nor is it to say that any one person sees or understands it all (including the CEO). The better-managed financial firms have organized the task of risk management so that expert views are gathered, edited, and summarized into a coherent and reasonable approximation of what is going on, allowing risk managers (including the CEO) to have a portfolio view of risk that, with a bit of luck, exposes all *major* risks to scrutiny and management and that identifies new opportunities to make money without taking excessive or unnecessary risks. Organizing for risk management also requires a careful assignment of authority and accountability for taking risks at all levels of the company.

Good risk management in banking, as I have described it, is not easy or cheap. Explicit, comprehensive, and *quantitative* risk management that actually shapes everyday decision making probably did not exist at all in any bank in the world before 1978, when we began to install the enterprise-wide risk assessment and risk management system (RAROC) at Bankers Trust, under the leadership of the chairman-to-be, Charlie Sanford. Nearly all of the world's banking regulators now have risk management requirements and guidelines that follow the spirit of what we did at Bankers Trust. Well-managed banks, in their own interest, are going well beyond what is minimally required by regulators.

Before we leave the banking world, let's fast forward one year to see how your risk decisions as CEO of ABC turned out.

EXAMPLE 4: THE RESULTS ARE IN

It is now one year later and we are looking up the current values of ABC's assets and liabilities in the *Wall Street Journal* so we can calculate the shareholders' net worth. It turns out that bond rates fell from 7 percent to 6.8 percent, causing the value of your bond position to increase from $2.000 billion to $2.050 billion. The Eurocurrency rate moved from 1.1 euros/dollar to 1.2 euros/dollar causing the value of your euro note position to fall from $1.000 billion to $917 million. The current value of our CD liability is $2.000 billion, because we have already paid its interest obligations and will, with certainty, pay back the principal of $2.000 billion tomorrow. After we mark the assets and liabilities to these current market values and put our net interest income on

Figure 7.16
ABC's Balance Sheet at Year End

Assets	Liabilities	Net Worth
$ 96 Cash	$2,000 CDs	
$2,050 Bonds		
$ 917 Euro Notes		
$3,063 Total	$2,000 Total	$1,063

the bonds and notes into cash, ABC's balance sheet looks like the one shown in Figure 7.16.

How did you do? You began the year with $1.000 billion in net worth and ended the year with $1.063 billion in net worth, so you made a profit of $63 million. First, the good news: You avoided the disaster scenario that you identified in your risk analysis and you made a profit for the year. Now, the bad news: Your return on shareholder equity was only 6.3 percent ($63/$1,000), *before* taxes or about 3 percent after taxes. This return is not much better than your investors would have earned if they had put their money in riskless passbook savings accounts rather than investing in ABC stock. For the amount of risk that you put on ABC's books, shareholders were expecting at least a 10 percent return *after tax* and probably more. You did not cover yourself with glory. But then the board tied your hands. Unless you can convince them to install an up-to-date risk management capability at ABC, you should consider resigning your position as CEO.

Chapter 8

YOU ARE IN CHARGE OF YOUR LIFE— WHAT ARE YOU GOING TO DO?

Now that you have left ABC Corporation with a nice fat severance package, you can turn your attention to the most important risk management challenge of all—your life. Not only do you have financial risks to manage similar to those at ABC, you have all the risks of everyday life that endanger your welfare. Risks to your property and possessions. Risks to success and satisfaction in your career. Risks to rewarding relationships with family and friends. Risks to your health and life. Risks to other people that you care about. Risks in all shapes and sizes coming from all directions. Risks that are vivid and compelling. Risks that are vague and ambiguous. Risks that are obscure or ignored. Risks that are immediate. Risks that are distant. Risks that are simply unknown.

Being entirely logical about all the risky decisions in your life would take the mother of all decision trees—millions of branches with trillions of possible outcomes. This problem is just too large and complex for anyone to give you a nice, neat risk management package to run your life. You need to consult your spiritual leader or favorite philosopher for that. As far as risk management has come, it is nowhere near such an elegant solution and probably never will be. Be deeply suspicious of anyone who tells you otherwise.

Also remember that human beings come hardwired with some very effective capabilities for dealing with risk that should not be overridden lightly. Our primitive ancestors dodged saber-toothed tigers, scavenged and hunted for scarce food, found shelter from extreme weather and learned to tell friend from foe. Over many millennia, humans developed instinctive responses to danger that allowed the fittest to survive and reproduce even fitter offspring. The most primitive of these is the well-known fight or flight response. At the first hint of danger, the fight or flight response takes over your mind and body to heighten alertness, to position the body for defense or attack, to release a flood of adrenaline to increase heart rate and muscle strength, and to command the lungs to increase their intake of oxygen. You are now primed and ready to attack or flee. The actual decision to fight or take flight is often made by the lower regions of the brain and is completely unconscious. When you come face to face with a grizzly bear, you don't have time to work out a decision tree. Your lack of logical rigor can be forgiven.

The dominance of instinct over logic is true of many of life's decisions. Your instinctive, unreasoned response is often best, or at least good enough. Step out of the way of that speeding bus. Don't entrust your life savings to a stranger on the phone. Hold on to the railing at the Grand Canyon visitor center. But this is not always the case. Instinctive responses work best in situations that resemble the environment in which they were developed—prehistoric forests, or jungles and savannas populated with small, scattered bands of people living off the land. Instinctive responses may not always work well in modern industrialized societies teeming with millions of people. Nor do they always take full advantage of the vast store of knowledge that human civilization has accumulated since people stopped living in trees. The fight or flight response can save you from a grizzly bear, but it can also get you thrown out of a bar and into jail. It can also give you a fatal heart attack at age 47. Suspicion of strangers can protect you from a mugger but it can also limit your opportunities to meet new friends and to find people who can help you. Looking to the evening sky to predict tomorrow's weather might work, but tuning in the Weather Channel is more reliable.

It is a wise person who knows when to trust her instincts and when to gather evidence, consult experts, and analyze the situation logically. *When the stakes are low,* instinct is fast, cheap, and usually good enough. If buying that pack of chewing gum feels right, just do it. *When time is short,* instinct may be the only way to decide in time. Remember the grizzly bear. Of course, if you have previously made a habit of trying to make informed and logical decisions, you may have stored up some useful knowledge and experience that can be called upon on short notice. The uniformed, natural instinct is to run from a grizzly, but holding your ground and acting confident may give you a better chance of survival. A park ranger would "instinctively" know this but a rookie camper would not. *When no conceivable decision has much effect on the outcome,* instinct saves you the trouble of pointless analysis. Choose any deck chair on the *Titanic.*

A more interesting case is *when the stakes are high enough to be important, there is some time available for analysis but fact-finding and logic are very difficult to apply.* The nature of the risks might be hard to identify and quantify. The menu of alternative decisions might be far from obvious. Your preferences for the possible outcomes may be hard to express clearly and consistently. Relevant information may be missing and hard to find. In situations such as these you are tempted to just rely on instinct, habit, or rules of thumb, because logical analysis seems so hard, so incomplete, and so inaccurate that it will not give you answers that you can trust. And in many cases, instinct, hopefully well informed by past experience, is the best way to make the decision.

EXAMPLE: MARRIAGE PROPOSAL

Deciding whether to get married is such a situation. The stakes are certainly high enough to be important. Extended periods of misery and possible financial ruin await those making bad choices. Unless we are talking about a shotgun wedding, there is time for some serious reflection. Most people spend months or even years with each other working up to the magic moment. But what is the decision tree for logically analyzing the risks of getting married to Mr. or Ms. Seemsright? Let's try to dream one up and see how far we get.

At first, identifying the alternative decisions seems easy. You can marry Ms. Seemsright or not marry her. But it is not that simple. Unless you are the absolute ruler of your own little country, you can't marry her if she doesn't want to marry you. You can only decide to *ask her* or *not ask her*. And when you ask her, don't you have to propose a *date* for the presumably happy event? Now, how many dates do you want to consider before proposing to her? Next week? Next month? Next year? Later? Much later? Since the possible consequences of asking to marry next week are different than the possible consequences of asking to marry next year, you need a branch of your decision tree for each possible marriage date if you want to be entirely logical.

We are in trouble already. Not only that, but we forgot some other alternatives: an immediate engagement announcement with an indefinite marriage date, living together but not marrying, or letting her decide the marriage date. You can probably think of other alternatives. Each alternative decision is likely to have a different set of possible consequences than the other alternatives and require its own branch on the decision tree.

But you are confident that the only decision alternatives worth analyzing are "Ask her to marry you six months from today" or "Don't ask her to marry you." Wait a minute—the "Don't ask" branch is not so simple either. Does "Don't ask" mean "Never ask" or "Don't ask now, but keep your options open to ask later" or "Tell her you want to break up"? See how this gets very complicated very soon?

You think about the options for a moment and decide that the only decision alternatives worth analyzing are "Ask her to marry you six months from today" or "Tell her that you want to break up." That simplifies your decision tree considerably but how do you know that you have not arbitrarily ruled out the best decision by failing to analyze it? You don't know, unless all the excluded decisions were clear losers with no prospect of being better than the decisions that you chose to analyze. You have to hope that your intuitive judgments are sound. And you have to remember that from here on, you have left the realm of pure logic and are operating in the realm of artfully combining logic and judgment.

Now it gets even harder. You have to identify all of the uncertain events and their possible consequences for both alternative decisions. Think about *that* for a minute. The first set of consequences for "Ask" is what Ms. Seemsright says in response to your proposal. She might keep things simple and say yes or no. But she might say "Maybe. Let me get back to you on that." What do you do next? You could respond "Okay, I'll wait for your answer." Or "I interpret hesitation as a lack of enthusiasm. Let's break up." If you decide to wait, how long will you wait and what will you do in the meantime? If you decide to break up, are you sure that you have correctly interpreted her attitude? Perhaps she is just being normally cautious about such a momentous decision even though she is enthusiastic about you as a person. By calling it quits, you may be throwing away a great opportunity that will not come again.

You think you know her well, so you are very confident that she will say either yes or no, but not "Maybe." So you won't include "Maybe" as a branch on your decision tree. Again you have simplified and again you can't be absolutely sure that you have not excluded the branch containing the best decision. But you are willing to trust your judgment on this decision.

Now you have to assess the possible consequences if she says yes and the possible consequences if she says no. If she says yes, one possible consequence would be children: How many? When? Boys or girls? Smart or dumb? Industrious or lazy? Healthy or sickly? Cheerful or phlegmatic? Virtuous or villainous? We could go on and on. Another consequence if she says yes would be companionship: Comforting or stressful? Stimulating or boring? Supportive or exhausting? Heaven or hell? Till death do we part or bitter divorce? Again we could go on and on. You can see that we are only scratching the surface here.

If she says no, what are the consequences? Well, what are you going to do if she says no? You have a decision tree within the decision tree. If you resolve to remain unmarried because your one true love has spurned you, you have one set of possible consequences. If you stay in the hunt, you have another and very different set of possible consequences, including the prospect of reliving this entire decision tree with another matrimonial candidate. If you commit suicide, you have the ultimate consequence, but a refreshingly simple branch of the decision tree.

This attempt to identify all of the possible consequences of all your alternative decisions is woefully incomplete and not going well at all, but let's slog through a bit more before we give up. Pretend that you have identified all the possible consequences of all the alternative decisions that you believe are worth analyzing. As you may remember, your next task is to assess the probability that each of these consequences will occur. What is the probability that Ms. Seemsright will say yes? If she says no, what is the probability that you will commit suicide?

And so on . . . and so on. Where do you get relevant data to assess these probabilities? I don't know, but you have to assess them anyway. Good luck.

It just keeps getting worse. Even after you have assessed all the probabilities required for the analysis, you are not done. You now have to assess your degree of preference (or utility) for each possible outcome (including death by suicide if she says no). Can you do that? Can we give up now?

The next time you hear someone criticize a happy couple for making an "overly emotional and illogical" decision to get married, you might run them through our example to give them some much-needed humility. They clearly don't have any idea of the impossible complexity and scale of analysis actually required for a "logical" decision about marriage. This argument does not advocate being capricious or willfully ignorant. Deciding whether to marry requires serious thought, but the decision must be made by relying primarily on judgment, common sense, instinct and, yes, emotion—and only secondarily on logical analysis. In any event, the mating process was so important to the survival and evolution of humans that it is still largely driven by hard-wired urges and behaviors passed on to us by our prehistoric ancestors and they are not likely to be overridden by a computer program any time soon.

Why have I dragged you through a painful example that clearly defeats the logical methods of risk analysis that are the main point of this book? There are two reasons.

First, the adoption of a useful tool like risk management can be slowed by overselling. When a risk management model fits the actual decision problem poorly and when the risk manager is unwilling or unable to overcome its shortcomings with sound judgment, bad decisions are made that unfairly damage the reputation of the risk management methods themselves. These same methods can be quite useful if applied properly and with good judgment. Many people would benefit from adopting the new risk management techniques and using them for decisions within their capabilities. We must use tools with an acute awareness of their limitations.

Second, even when a formal risk management model fails to be realistic enough to give answers that can be trusted on their own, the process of trying to construct the model often helps you make better judgments and therefore better decisions. In going through the decision tree drill, you may identify decision alternatives and uncertain events that you might have otherwise overlooked. You may discover unexpected links between different events (such as correlation). As you think hard about the probabilities of events, you may change your view of which events are really important to your decision and which are less important or even irrelevant. You may clarify your objectives as you try to be specific about your preferences for different outcomes. Even though your attempt to build a sufficiently realistic decision tree may fail, you will almost always be better off trying than if you had just winged it. Unless, of course, you come across that grizzly bear in the woods.

EXAMPLE: FAT OR LEAN?

It is possible that our marriage proposal decision tree got to be unmanageably messy because we were trying to be too detailed and precise. Perhaps in such decisions we could do better by taking a broader view—look at the forest, not the trees. Let's try that approach with another fundamental life decision—whether to sacrifice enjoyment of food for the prospect of a longer life.

Suppose that you love gourmet cooking. You love eggs, butter, cheese, cream, sugar, salt, and red meat and you especially love the way a fine French chef can combine them all into a heavenly meal. You also worry that such heavenly meals will send you to heaven sooner than if you followed a less sclerotic diet. You have looked at some medical research and you believe that your gourmet diet is reducing your expected life span by increasing the probability that you will die from a heart attack, from stroke, from diabetes, or from some other diet-related fatal malady.

You have a basic decision to make: Indulge your gourmet tastes or eat sensibly. This decision is extremely important because your choice has a dramatic effect on the outcome, so you want to be as logical as you can. You begin to construct a simple decision tree.

You assess your probability beliefs for the potential life spans associated with each lifestyle. You not only look at the averages in the medical journals, but you adjust for your age, sex, and current health. Not bad for an amateur biostatistician.

Everything else being equal, you prefer a longer life to a shorter life. But everything else is not equal. You also care deeply about the *quality* of your life under each scenario. Gourmet living makes your life, however short, happy. Lean living makes your life, however long, dull. So there are *two* attributes that determine your utility for the outcomes of this decision: remaining life span—long, average or short; and quality of life—happy or dull.

You now climb to the mountaintop for a period of deep introspection (don't forget to pack a nice lunch). When you return, you have quantified your preferences for all the possible outcomes and are ready to show me your decision tree as shown in Figure 8.1.

Figure 8.1
Decision Tree: Fat or Lean?

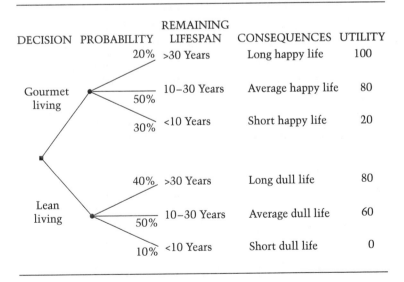

DECISION	PROBABILITY	REMAINING LIFESPAN	CONSEQUENCES	UTILITY
Gourmet living	20%	>30 Years	Long happy life	100
	50%	10–30 Years	Average happy life	80
	30%	<10 Years	Short happy life	20
Lean living	40%	>30 Years	Long dull life	80
	50%	10–30 Years	Average dull life	60
	10%	<10 Years	Short dull life	0

You believe that a lean lifestyle doubles your chances of living an unusually long life (40 percent versus 20 percent) and that a gourmet lifestyle triples your chance of an early death (30 percent versus 10 percent). But a lean lifestyle does not guarantee a long life (you might be hit by a beer truck). Nor does a gourmet lifestyle dictate a short life (you might have unusually good genes or further research may reveal that crème brûlée is actually good for you).

The best outcome for you would be the long, happy life that is only possible with a gourmet lifestyle. You assign that outcome a utility of 100. The worst outcome would be the short, dull life that can happen only under a lean lifestyle. You assign that outcome a utility of zero. Some people might prefer a short, dull life to a long, dull life, but they are not the decision makers here, you are.

The other outcomes require you to weigh life span against happiness. You are indifferent between a long, dull life and an average happy life (you assigned a utility of 80 to each). But you prefer either an average dull life (utility of 60) or a long, dull life (utility of 80) to a short happy, life (utility of 20). You are not a completely myopic hedonist.

You are now ready to make your decision. Note that neither the probabilities, by themselves, nor the utilities, by themselves, are sufficient to tell you what is the best decision. You must consider them together and choose the lifestyle that maximizes your expected utility. The expected utility of a gourmet lifestyle is:

$$.20 \times 100 + .50 \times 80 + .30 \times 20 = \mathbf{66}$$

The expected utility of a lean lifestyle is:

$$.40 \times 80 + .50 \times 60 + .10 \times 0 = \mathbf{62}$$

You are now permitted to indulge yourself because you have made a completely rational decision to pursue a gourmet lifestyle. The expected utility of pigging out is greater than the expected utility of eating tofu. Of course, you might change your mind later as new evidence rolls in or as the grim reaper draws nearer. Or you might be troubled by the utter simplicity of our approach. Have we swept too much under the rug? Only you can decide.

A PORTFOLIO VIEW OF YOUR RISKS

Just as we did when you were CEO of ABC Bank, we would like you to be able to see the full panorama of the risks that you are taking at any one time. We want you to see their size and how they might relate to one another. We want to reduce the chance that you overlook an important risk or opportunity. We want to increase the chance that you can see ways to trade one risk against another or to shed or acquire risks that improve overall balance of risk and potential benefit in your aggregate risk position.

I am not aware of any widely accepted way of doing this for a human being's risk position. There are many financial planning models but they cover only one part of just the financial dimension of risk. We want a much more expansive view. In the end, we will fail to be sufficiently realistic because human life has too many complexities and uncertainties. Remember the example of the marriage proposal where we had to give up before we found a way to realistically capture just one of life's important decisions. Or the example of fat or lean, where we could construct a decision tree but that tree might have been oversimplified. But the effort to be rational and systematic is worthwhile because we should learn something from it that will help us make better decisions in real life.

If we cannot hope to manage your personal risks rigorously by a monster decision tree, what do we do? One approach to a comprehensive risk management system for your personal life might be to proceed as if you were a corporation. We already know that risk management techniques can be very useful in a corporate setting, allowing managers to make better decisions than they would have made relying solely on gut feel and rules of thumb alone. Maybe we can make similar methods work in your personal life. Unfortunately, we will not succeed in this either, but we might learn something from trying.

Despite knowing that we will fail, let's start by constructing your personal balance sheet, which purports to tell you where you stand at any given moment. The corporate balance sheet of Chapter 7 is shown here as Figure 8.2.

Let's assume that the same principle applies to your personal balance sheet (see Figure 8.3), even when we include nonfinancial as well as financial items. (Remember this assumption.) To reflect this broader view, we use the term "well-being," rather

Figure 8.2
Balance Sheet

| What You Own | Minus | What You Owe | Equals | What You Can Keep |
| Assets | Minus | Liabilities | Equals | Net Worth |

than net worth. As the philosophers tell us, financial net worth is only one part of well-being.

Your personal assets include anything that you possess that can give you satisfaction (or utility) now or in the future, such as

- *Financial assets.* Cash, checking and savings accounts, stocks, bonds, mutual funds, 401(k) plans, pension plans, insurance policies, lottery tickets, IOUs from Cousin Harold, and. . . .
- *Physical assets.* Houses, cars, boats, furniture and appliances, clothing, art, stamp collections, family photos, souvenirs, heirlooms, and. . . .
- *Intellectual assets.* Knowledge, skills, talents, intelligence, inventions, ideas, creativity, reputation, professional licenses and credentials, network of business contacts, and. . . .

Figure 8.3
Personal Balance Sheet

| Personal Assets | Minus | Personal Liabilities | Equals | Well-Being |

- *Emotional assets.* Good physical and mental health, rewarding relationships with family and friends, free time, access to entertaining or stimulating activities, ability to win friends and influence people, inner peace (however it may be attained), and. . . .

Your personal liabilities include anything that can require you to give up satisfaction now or in the future, such as

- *Financial liabilities.* Mortgages, car loans, credit card debt, student loans, bills payable, taxes payable, alimony, gambling debts, and. . . .
- *Physical liabilities.* Borrowed lawnmower, and. . . .
- *Intellectual liabilities.* Necessity to spend time providing labor or services or to spend time acquiring new skills and knowledge.
- *Emotional liabilities.* Necessity to endure physical pain or emotional angst, obligations to spend time with boring, aggravating, or otherwise unpleasant people.

So now we have the means to sum up the entire value of your life in one number: well-being, which equals personal assets minus personal liabilities. We could adopt a specific, quantifiable definition of personal risk: the reduction in well-being that could occur with a given probability within a given period of time. Personal risk is analogous to the value-at-risk (VaR) methods used by corporations. By assessing the possible changes in value of your personal assets and liabilities, we could assess the risks and opportunities of different decisions and scenarios for your life. These scenarios would capture any links (or correlation) among the changes in value of each personal asset or liability with the changes in value of every other personal asset or liability. You could view the entire panorama of the risks that you face as a human being. You could improve your risk exposure by shedding or acquiring personal assets or liabilities. You could run your life as if it were a well-managed corporation. You could have an annual meeting.

Just kidding. I have gone way beyond what is currently possible or even appropriate. For example, you may have noticed that I skipped the rather important step of *quantifying the values* of all your personal assets and personal liabilities. If I had successfully done so, I would be in the running for the Greatest Philosopher of All Time Award. Financial assets and liabilities are relatively easy to value in *monetary* terms. Look up your stocks at the Yahoo! Finance web site. Physical assets and liabilities are harder, but certainly can be done with reasonable accuracy. Take your old lamp to the Antiques Road Show. Intellectual assets and liabilities are much harder but not impossible because they ultimately result in financial flows, which can be estimated within a broad range of accuracy. There are experts who testify to "lifetime earnings potential" in personal injury cases. Of course, intellectual assets produce more than financial flows. They can produce satisfaction directly without producing money first. Read a good book. So the value of the prospective financial flows produced by intellectual assets is a lower bound on their total value. This method works better for Bill Gates than it does for the Dalai Lama.

When we get to emotional assets and liabilities, we have serious quantification problems, to say the least. For example, most people recoil at the thought of putting a monetary value on their relationships with friends and family. If pressed they will say "priceless," or perhaps "worthless." Of course, they *implicitly* value these relationships if they spend time away from friends and family to earn money that does not improve their relationships with friends and family.

Things really get sticky when people are asked to quantify the value of saving a life. If it is a family member, they may give up all they have to save that life, including sacrificing their own life. However, as the relationship grows more distant, the willingness to pay out of one's own pocket drops rather sharply. From the distant view of society at large, the willingness to pay to save an individual life is often not very great and depends on factors that have little or nothing to do with the intrinsic value of the life in question. An immediate and obvious threat to an identifiable person is more likely to get attention and money than is a vague or distant threat to many people in general but no one in particular. The Coast Guard spends thousands of dollars to rescue one person from a sinking sailboat. But a local government fails to increase the mosquito spraying budget despite a much wetter than normal spring. The officials know that one or two additional citizens are highly likely to die of West Nile virus as a result of the inadequate spraying. But they don't know who, they don't know when, and they don't know if they would have died anyway, because no amount of spraying is 100 percent effective. And because they are engaged in an act of omission rather than commission, they are far less likely to be blamed by others or to feel guilty themselves.

Are these calculations right or wrong? Rational or irrational? Moral or immoral? Whatever they may be, the answers to these kinds of calculations depend very much on the point of view of the person doing the calculating. But let the social and political scientists worry about that. Since you are the risk manager for your own life it is only your valuations that matter when you are making decisions on your own behalf.

As hard as these asset and liability values are to assess, a more fundamental difficulty is the very assumption that units of well-being can be expressed in monetary terms and that they can be added and subtracted to get the net well-being produced by a scenario or a decision. Remember that we already know how to solve our problem in a fully rational way. We need to construct a monster decision tree with all the decisions and all the probabilities, outcomes, and utilities of all the uncertain events flowing from those decisions. We then do the math to find the set of decisions that produces the highest expected utility. Our personal balance sheet calculations are not very likely to give us the same answers as the monster decision tree. But we also know that the monster decision tree is wildly impractical to actually do. That is why we tried to apply corporate risk management methods to your personal risk position.

But our corporate model fails at the personal level because it assumes that monetary values are all that matter. For a corporation, monetary values are fungible; they can be added, subtracted, and traded off against each other, no matter where they came from. This assumption is not bad for a corporation because it is an economic entity whose sole purpose is to make money. This assumption *is* bad for a human being because rational human beings should care about *utility*, not money in and of itself. Money can provide utility but so can clean air, a Mozart concerto, and a coy wink from an attractive dinner companion.

So where are we? We do not have any practical and appropriate method for analyzing your entire risk portfolio as a human being and for telling you what decisions are best for you. Monster decision trees are rigorous and rational, but impractical. Corporate risk management techniques are practical but focus on the wrong objectives for a rational human being.

Fortunately, all is not lost. You will muddle through with partial solutions, approximations, guesses and, most of all, good judgment. You will break down the monster problem into smaller problems where decision trees or other risk management techniques can actually be of practical help. You will use the results of these models as part of the solution, as steps toward the solution, and as tools to help you think more clearly about your problem. Then you will take a leap of judgment and make your decision. You will never take the output of models as final answers to be acted upon without further thought.

The value of risk management is not to give you easy answers to hard problems but to help you think more clearly and therefore make better decisions than you would otherwise have made. Many people are trying to sell you easy answers to hard problems: Lose 30 pounds and eat whatever you like! Become rich in 30 days working at home! Find the man of your dreams by sweetening your breath! Never believe such people. And never believe anyone with a risk management model or set of rules that purports to tell you the right choices for important decisions in your life without understanding your life. You are the risk manager of your own life and you must use your own judgment in applying advice and information supplied by others, however qualified they may be. No insurance agent, no lawyer, no accountant, no stockbroker, no financial planner, no doctor, no guru of any kind has a prepackaged solution completely right for you. Do they understand your preferences for different outcomes? Do they know your probability beliefs for uncertain events? Consider their advice if you trust their competence and honesty but take it as useful input, not as the final answer. The final answer can only come from you. The examples we just went through should have convinced you that easy answers to hard problems are likely to be wrong.

Even though we have to give up, for now, the grandiose dream of having a complete risk management model for your life, we can explore some examples of applying risk management techniques to some of life's decisions. We know that our models are incomplete at best, but they may help you think more clearly about the problems.

EXAMPLE: HOME INSURANCE

You own a house with a current market value of $400,000. To rebuild the same house on the same site would cost $325,000. The contents of the house (furniture and other possessions) would cost $100,000 to replace. Like most people you are worried that your house and possessions could be damaged or lost by fire, flood, wind, or other hazards, so you want insurance to protect you. Your insurance agent says that he is willing to sell you up to $425,000 of coverage for your house and possessions for an annual premium of $2,000. The policy will pay 90 percent of all damages up to a maximum of $425,000 with a cumulative annual deductible of $5,000.

But should you buy insurance? Is it worth the premium being charged? Most people get at least a mild headache when trying to think logically about these kinds of decisions. It can be very confusing. The easy way out is to get several quotes from reputable companies and pick the cheapest policy that gives you enough coverage to make you feel comfortable. If you live in an area where there are many insurance companies freely competing for your business, taking the easy way out is probably not a bad way to make the decision (unless you rashly conclude that you need no insurance at all). You will probably get a decent price for the coverage that you buy. It is not clear that intensive analysis is worth the trouble. But if you wanted to be as rational as you could, you would construct a decision tree that included your beliefs about the probabilities of damage and loss and your preferences (or utility) for various levels of loss.

Let's walk through the process of doing your decision tree. First, you assess your probability beliefs. You surf the internet looking for loss histories on properties like yours in areas like yours. Losses come mainly from fire, flood, earthquake, wind and rain storms, and theft. Fortunately, your policy would cover them all (this is not always the case). Data readily applicable to your particular property is hard to find, but you take what you have and use *your judgment* to come up with *your own beliefs* about the amounts and probabilities of combined losses, within one year, from all sources. This is not easy to do unless you are an actuary, but that is too bad. You have to try it if you want to be rational.

After some arduous thought, you believe that there is a 99 percent probability that you will have no loss or damage within the year, there is a 0.8 percent probability that you will have $75,000 of losses within the year, and there is a .2 percent probability that you will have a complete disaster that causes $425,000 of damage and loss within the year.

Next you must calculate the consequences of all the possible scenarios. If you don't buy insurance and a loss occurs, you absorb the entire loss but if no loss occurs, your net loss is zero.

If you buy insurance and no loss occurs, your net loss is $2,000, the insurance premium. But if a loss occurs, your net loss is the [insurance premium] plus [damages] minus [insurance claim = .90 × damage up to $425,000 – deductible]. So if losses are $425,000, the net loss is 2,000 + 425,000 – [.9 × $425,000 – 5,000] = $49,500.

Finally, you must assess your preferences (or utility) for all the possible consequences. As we have done before, to help you assess your utility curve, I ask you the following question:

> Suppose I offered you the following gamble: I flip a coin and if it comes up heads, you win $100,000. But if it comes up tails, you lose $50,000. In other words, you have a 50 percent chance of winning $100,000 and a 50 percent chance of losing $50,000. How much would you pay me for the opportunity to take this gamble?

This gamble has a positive expected value of $25,000 (.50 × 100 + .50 × (–50)). If you were able to take this gamble 100 times in a row you would be highly likely to win about $2.5 million (100 × $25,000). This gamble is much, much better than any gamble you will find in Las Vegas or in the state lottery. If you gamble repeatedly at Las Vegas or in the lottery, you are highly likely to lose money, because such gambles have *negative* expected values.

Now you think carefully about how you would feel if you won $100,000 and how you would feel if you lost $50,000. Then you say "I would pay you $20,000 for the opportunity to take that gamble."

It may seem very adventurous to risk losing a net $70,000 in order to have an equal chance of winning a net $80,000, but you are still being risk averse. If you were indifferent to risk, you would have been willing to pay me up to $25,000 to play.

Because you are risk averse, you will often be willing to give up some upside in order to reduce your downside. The pain of losing $10,000 is greater than the pleasure of winning $10,000. You will be willing to pay for peace of mind even if it costs you some potential upside. You are a good prospect for an insurance agent. But don't feel embarrassed for being too timid. I would not pay $20,000 for that gamble so I am much more risk averse than you are. Your self-image as an aggressive risk taker is not in danger.

To complete the assessment of your utility function, I show you several more gambles with different gains and losses and ask you to tell me how much you would pay me for each. From your answers, I can construct the utility curve appropriate for your current situation. We can assign utility values to each outcome on your decision tree.

Now you have everything that you need to complete your decision tree (Figure 8.4).

Looking at your decision tree, we see that you believe that there is a 1 percent probability (.8 percent + .2 percent) of experiencing significant damage or loss within the year ($75,000 or $425,000) and a 99 percent chance of experiencing no damage at all. The chance of damage is very small, but if damage occurs it will be unpleasant ($75,000) or disastrous ($425,000). If you buy insurance, the worst case is a net loss of $49,500 including the $2,000 cost of the premium on the policy. For a known cost up front ($2,000), you

Figure 8.4
Decision Tree for Buying Homeowner's Insurance

DECISION	PROBABILITY	DAMAGE	NET LOSS	UTILITY
	99%	$(0)	$(2)	.9993551
Buy insurance	0.8%	$(75)	$(14.5)	.9952646
	0.2%	$(425)	$(49.5)	.9832250
	99%	$(0)	$(0)	1.0000000
Do not buy insurance	0.8%	$(75)	$(75)	.9738489
	0.2%	$(425)	$(425)	.6947322

substantially reduce your worst case loss from $425,000 to $49,500 if you buy insurance.

Notice that your decision tree states that the probabilities and amounts of potential damage are the same whether you buy the insurance policy or not. This is evidence of your honesty and diligence. The insurance company would be very upset to discover that you believed damage claims were much more likely or potentially much larger if you bought the policy than if you did not. They might, for example, suspect that you were intending to slack off on fire prevention or fake a burglary. Insurance companies take such a dim view of this behavior that they have a buzz ard. They go to great lengths to avoid moral hazards—situations where the insured party has the ability and motivation to increase the amount or probability of insurance claims, whether through fraud or carelessness. One way to discourage carelessness is to make sure that the insured party experiences at least some loss, through deductibles or copayments, if a claim is made. One way to discourage fraud is to have claims adjusters that verify the amount of actual damages and their cause so that they can send people to jail who make false claims.

You also believe there is a 99 percent chance that your policy won't pay off because no damage or loss will have occurred during the year. If so, have you wasted the $2,000 premium? Not necessarily, because you bought one year's worth of peace of mind that might have been worth even more to you than its $2,000 cost. That is what most insurance decisions amount to: How much are you willing to pay for peace of mind?

To help you think about the value to you of buying this insurance, we calculate your *expected value* of loss if you don't buy insurance.

$$.99 \times \$0 + .008 \times \$75,000 + .002 \times \$425,000 = -\$1,450$$

Calculating your *expected value* of loss if you *do* buy insurance, we get:

$$.99 \times \$2,000 + .008 \times \$14,500 + .002 \times \$49,500 = -\$2,195$$

Wait a minute! Your expected value of loss is *higher* if you buy insurance than if you do not buy insurance. Why would you buy insurance? Because the utility function you used in your decision tree implies that you are risk averse and you are not indifferent between two gambles with the same expected values but with different downsides. You want to avoid the gamble with the higher downside and you are willing to give up some expected value to do so. So you choose the strategy that has the highest expected utility.

The expected utility of buying insurance is:

$$.99 \times (.9993551) + .008 \times (.9952646) + .002 \times (.9832250) = .9992901$$

The expected utility of not buying insurance is:

$$.99 \times (1.0) + .008 \times (.9738489) + .002 \times (.6947322) = .9991803$$

To you, the potential pain of losing $425,000 is so great, even though it is highly unlikely, that buying this insurance policy is a better decision than not buying it. The answer might be different if your probability beliefs implied much lower potential losses, if you were much less risk averse, or if the insurance premiums were much higher.

For example, if you had been willing to pay me nearly $25,000 for that first gamble that I offered you, you would be less risk averse and your expected utility of buying insurance would be less than your expected utility of not buying insurance. Therefore you would not buy the insurance. Or if the insurance policy cost $3,000 rather than $2,000, you would conclude that the peace of mind produced by the insurance policy was not enough to justify buying the policy.

Notice that the insurance company proposes to charge you $2,000 for a policy that has expected losses of only $1,450 (according to *your* beliefs). Is this fair? You know that the insurance company will be writing thousands of these policies all over the country. If the claims on these policies are independent (or uncorrelated) with each other, the insurance company's portfolio of claims will be highly diversified and most of the uncertainty about portfolio losses will be eliminated—the actual loss will be very close to the expected loss. If the company wrote 100,000 policies just like yours, its losses would be close to $145 million ($1,450 × 100,000). If the company has done a good job of estimating the probabilities of loss on each policy, it would be quite unlikely that it would lose much more or less than this. So if it prices its premiums to collect at least $145 million, it is quite likely to at least break even on its underwriting of the policies. But it also has to cover its administrative and sales expenses and make a fair profit for its shareholders. So a fair profit for the insurance company implies that you should expect to pay more in premiums than the *insurance company* expects to pay out on your policy. Up to a point, you are willing to pay more than the expected loss because you are risk averse and because you have no other way to get rid of the risk. The insurance company has a risk reduction method that you do not have and you are willing to pay for using it for your benefit.

If the insurance company does not actually achieve a diversified portfolio or if it misjudges the level of risk on many individual policies, it could fail to make a profit or even lose money. In fact, property and casualty losses have proved to be difficult to estimate accurately and insurance companies in that business have posted surprisingly large underwriting losses in some years (as in hurricane Andrew).

The foregoing is just one example of how risk management methods can be used in your personal life to help you make better decisions. Explicit risk management can be very helpful in decisions where the financial dimension dominates, like investing in the stock market. Sophisticated financial planners are using detailed simulations of the consequences of different investment programs under different financial market scenarios. They are also getting better at assessing and using their client's particular risk preferences in deciding how to invest the client's money.

One of the more exciting developments is the application of decision theory to medical decisions: whether to operate, whether to use radiation therapy, whether to prescribe a drug. There is a vast and growing store of evidence available on the frequencies of different medical outcomes in different circumstances that can be the starting point for populating a decision tree with probabilities.

As we have already seen, a more difficult issue is specifying preferences (utilities) for the outcomes.

Whose preferences? The patient's? The doctor's? The HMO's? The government's? Who is the decision maker when so many are involved and when so many legitimate, but competing interests are at stake? When you are about to be wheeled into the operating room, your natural inclination is to put your personal interests first. And you should do just that when you have to make a decision about your medical treatment. But all the decisions will not be made by you. In fact, many of the most important decisions will be made by someone else. Will they take your beliefs and preferences into account when they decide what will and will not be done for you?

And most difficult, how do we put a utility on life or death itself? We do it every day, of course, by making decisions that affect the probabilities of life and death, whether our own or that of someone else. But these judgments are implicit, often invisible, and do not draw the scrutiny or accountability that an explicit judgment would draw. This is unfortunate because explicit, rational judgments are likely to lead to better decisions.

EXAMPLE: TAKE TWO TPAs AND CALL ME IN THE MORNING

The following example of using decision theory in making a medical decision is based on "Comparison of Accelerated Tissue Plasminogen Activator with Streptokinase for Treatment of Suspected Myocardial Infarction" by J. Kellet and J. Clarke (*Medical Decision Making*, vol. 15 [1995], pp. 297–310).

A patient having a heart attack might be saved by early administration of drugs that inhibit blood clotting, including tissue plasminogen activator (TPA), streptokinase, or common aspirin. However, such drugs can sometimes cause fatal hemorrhaging or a fatal or debilitating stroke. To aid in deciding which drug should be used to treat a patient, Kellet and Clarke constructed the decision tree that is shown in Figure 8.5.

Given the probabilities and utilities assumed in Figure 8.5, the best treatment decision is to use TPA for it has the highest expected utility despite its possible side effects. But for a patient who is less likely to be actually experiencing a heart attack, the results are different. For example, if you believe that there is only a 17 percent chance that the patient is having a heart attack, treating with aspirin alone has the highest expected utility.

I am not a doctor or medical researcher, so I can't pass judgment on the decisions considered, the possible outcomes, or the probabilities of the outcomes. And as we know, utilities are a strictly personal matter. You may or may not assign a .5 utility to a debilitating stroke, but if you find yourself in the ambulance, it is unlikely that the paramedics will attempt to assess your utility curve. Nevertheless, such an analysis can be very instructive to those who will have to make the decision for you. It helps them to make better use of the information and experience that they have, which should lead to more effective treatments. And in other situations, like elective surgery, going through a decision tree might help you make a better-informed decision for

Figure 8.5
Decision Tree for Treatment of Possible Heart Attack

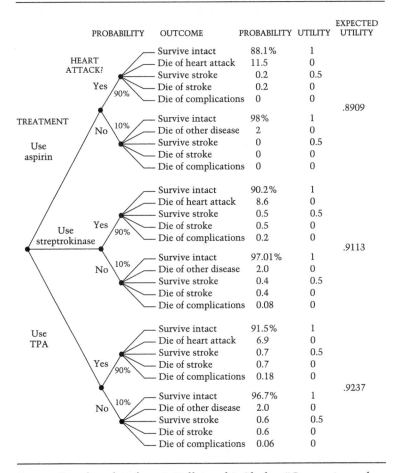

Source: Based on data from J. Kellet and J. Clarke, "Comparison of accelerated tissue plasminogen activator with streptokinase for treatment of suspected myocardial infarction," *Medical Decision Making*, vol. 15 (1995), pp. 297–310.

yourself. You may feel more comfortable with and in greater control of what is going on.

The use of rigorous risk management techniques to make important decisions in personal life is still in its early days. Some decisions may always lie beyond these methods, particularly those—such as marriage and family relationships—that are, *and should be*, inextricably entangled with instinctive behaviors and emotions. But whenever we can benefit from better information and sounder logic, risk management techniques can be powerful tools to help us decide what to do.

Chapter 9

RISKS AND OPPORTUNITIES

I hope that you agree by now that there is a potentially better way to make important decisions about risk than simply relying on instinct, intuition, habit, rules of thumb, or "the way that it is done around here." Trying to be explicitly logical about alternative decisions, uncertain events, probability beliefs, and preferences can clarify your objectives and your understanding of the risks and opportunities that you face. In many cases, the process of applying these risk management techniques can suggest much better decisions than those that would have otherwise occurred to you.

I hope that you also agree by now that as powerful as risk management techniques can be, you must use them with judgment—judgment that appreciates and compensates for the limitations of risk management models in particular settings. Good risk management is not a branch of artificial intelligence or expert systems, for the goal is not to replace the human brain but to extend its reach and amplify its power.

Throughout this book, I have tried to cast you in the role of the decision maker so that you could appreciate the potential power of risk management from that perspective. In fact, *risk management is designed expressly for decision makers*—people who must decide what to do in uncertain situations where time is short and information is incomplete and who will experience real consequences from their decision.

Chief executive officers (CEOs), doctors, bankers, investors, owners of small businesses, judges, presidents, kings, army generals, airline pilots, police, and paramedics are in professions that require them to make important decisions in uncertain situations. All of them can benefit from better risk management. Even if you are not a professional decision maker, you have many important decisions to make in your personal life. You too can benefit from better risk management.

The role of decision maker is special. A scientist investigates, speculates, and suspends final judgment to wait for better theories or better data. This process is entirely appropriate when the goal is to search for truth, but a decision maker cannot wait to decide (unless he *decides* to wait). An advisor provides information and may suggest possible decisions and scenarios but does not have to choose among them and will not feel the full force of their consequences.

For a decision maker, the necessity to act focuses the mind and arouses the gut in a way that advising or fact-finding does not. Remember that grizzly bear in the woods? A decision maker is on the hook and has to confront and resolve ambiguity as best he can in the time available. Decision making is stressful. To avoid this stress, we may deny, dismiss, postpone, pass the buck, or defer to higher authority. Or we may default to habit, custom, or rules. A responsible decision maker cannot use any of these escape hatches. A risk management framework is just what that decision maker needs because it is a tool that allows ambiguity to be confronted and resolved by transforming it into alternatives, events, beliefs, and preferences that can be analyzed logically.

Despite its rapid growth, the explicit practice of modern risk management has penetrated only a small fraction of its potential applications. It is not an easy discipline for an aspiring risk manager to learn, for it requires a new way of thinking. People with risk management skills are in short supply. It is not an easy discipline for an organization to implement because it requires much more than just data and analysis. It requires changing the way the organization makes decisions and sometimes changing the people who make them. Old ways of doing things are rarely abandoned with enthusiasm. Change creates fear and fear creates resistance.

If good risk management is so difficult, why bother? One reason is defensive. The world is getting more competitive, interconnected, and complex. Events seem more unpredictable and are moving with greater speed and force. Many of the old safety nets enjoyed by organizations and individuals are badly frayed or gone altogether. The level and nature of risks in the world are constantly changing. Those without access to good risk management are in greater danger than before.

For example, financial institutions have lost much of the protection from competition that governments had formerly granted them. Interest rates, exchange rates, commission rates, and most other terms of doing business are now largely unregulated. The barriers to doing financial business across national borders are much lower. The distinctions between different types of financial institutions are rapidly fading. Commercial banks, brokers, investment banks, investment advisors, and insurance companies have lost their formerly crisp identities and their areas of protected turf. Financial conglomerates now do all these things and more. Financial firms are engaged in so many businesses in so many places that the sheer complexity of their risk profiles is staggering. Those without good risk management capabilities are relying solely on naïve diversification to keep them out of serious trouble. Maybe it will but more likely it will not. Sooner or later an unrecognized correlation across many of their activities will give them a nasty surprise.

The financial markets themselves are more numerous and more interconnected than ever. Shocks in one market can quickly spread to other markets. Prices may spike up or down without warning and without apparent reason. Liquidity may dry up at the worst possible moment. Investors and others relying on the financial markets cannot afford to be ignorant of the risks that they may be taking or to be unprepared to take action to protect themselves.

Businesses are subject to greater competition from all over the globe. Governments, in an admittedly haphazard fashion, have lowered many barriers to international trade that once sheltered domestic companies from competition. Unexpected changes in currency rates or labor costs can make overseas goods more competitive and endanger the profits of domestic companies. Innovation is accelerating. A new invention can make existing products obsolete with frightening speed. Better-informed customers are becoming more demanding and more price-sensitive so that brand loyalty does not have the power that it once had. New competitors with unconventional ways of doing business can rapidly erode the market share of traditional firms. Those who feel wronged by a corporation's behavior are much more likely to take their grievance to the courts or regulators. A business firm without good risk management is much more likely to be blindsided by unexpected shifts in product markets and client behavior, unfavorable regulation or legal action, operating blunders or competitive threats.

Even governments are not immune from rising pressures to manage themselves better. The global capital markets now exert considerable discipline on the economic policies of sovereign countries. Countries that have poor business climates, stifling regulation, wasteful public spending, burdensome taxation, excessive money creation, or other policies that do not please investors find that their access to vital external capital is restricted or priced unfavorably. The bond trader has replaced the Hun as the most fearsome threat to poorly managed countries. The spread of democracy in Russia, Eastern Europe, Latin America, and elsewhere has created pressures for higher economic growth, redistribution of wealth, better education and health care, a larger role for the private sector, more accountability for public institutions, greater respect for human rights, and greater freedom to make a living and to live in the way that one chooses. None of these things are easy for a government to do and the risks of failure are great. A government must explicitly recognize these risks and try to manage them openly and rationally.

Finally, individuals have lost the safety nets that once promised to protect them from adversity. Social Security in the United States is no longer counted on to provide an adequate level of income in old age. The promised benefits are too low and the very solvency of the system is in doubt. Pension plans are shifting from providing defined benefits to providing defined contributions, leaving it up to individuals to choose their own investments and to bear the full risk of those investments. The social contract between workers and corporations has changed fundamentally. Once, a loyal and competent worker expected to be able to work for his company for life. No longer. Corporations do not expect worker loyalty and do not offer lifetime employment. They cannot even offer the promise of continued corporate existence. The worker is now a free agent and will presumably leave if offered a better deal elsewhere. The company can restructure, downsize, streamline, or reengineer at will. Job security is a relic of the past. Your career is not tied to the company who you happen to be working for but to the knowledge in your head and the names in your Rolodex. Outside of work, the support and comfort provided by belonging to a community is harder to find. Small towns and close-knit neighborhoods have been swept away by urban sprawl that is ugly and impersonal. People in need have fewer friends or family nearby to help them out. Medical science marches on but the health care system is growing more complex, more expensive, and more impersonal. Patients are often treated as lab experiments or potential litigants rather than as whole human beings. In today's world, individuals are on their own and must take charge of their own risks because there is no longer anyone there to do it for them.

The defensive motive for good risk management is abundantly clear but just as it is foolish to ignore these risks, it is also foolish to be too cautious. Businesses and financial institutions may hold excessive capital to buffer risks or may pass up investments that would strengthen their competitive positions. Individuals may be so timid in their choice of investments that they fail to build the wealth that they need for their financial security. Governments may not make the investments necessary to build a sounder economic and social system or may stifle innovation and progress by regulations that overly restrict risk taking by their citizens and businesses.

As we have said before, the goal of good risk management is not to minimize risk but to achieve the best balance of risk and opportunity. Many of the foregoing threats are also opportunities if you have the ability to seize them and turn them to your advantage. Risk management can help you do that.

Financial institutions and business corporations can use active risk management to reinforce their strategies and build shareholder value. At a tactical level, a firm can change its exposure to interest rates, currency rates, oil prices, copper prices, electricity prices, and a host of other variables. Sometimes the purpose is to reduce or eliminate an exposure because it is extraneous to the core business. It will only contribute volatility that obscures the results of the core business and diverts management attention. In the extreme, the extraneous exposure can cause a serious accident that derails the company. But sometimes the purpose is to increase or acquire an exposure because the company believes it has a competitive advantage in forecasting how that market will move. If the company is right, it can profit by being in the business of buying and selling that type of exposure.

At a strategic level, we know that a firm is a complex portfolio of business and financial risks. The results from this aggregate portfolio determine the success or failure of the company. The top management of the firm, especially the CEO, can view and manage this portfolio as a whole, trading off one risk against another, reducing risks that are peripheral to the company's long-term strategy, or adding risks (and opportunities) that are central to that strategy. Strategic risk management can help a business achieve its primary business goals without endangering its financial stability.

For example, imagine that your company acquired an equity interest in a high-tech startup several years ago in order to gain production and marketing rights to an exciting new technology. The value of that equity investment has surged to over $500 million. Unfortunately, the tech stock market is extremely volatile and you would like to shed that volatility— after all, you are an industrialist not a professional stock market investor. You could sell the investment but selling such a large position would be expensive and time consuming. More importantly, selling would disrupt your relationship with your strategic partner, possibly shutting you out of vital new technology developments that represent the highest growth sector of your core business. Because you understand the business from the inside, you are also bullish in the long term about your strategic partner's stock and don't want to sacrifice that potential payoff. What can you do? Using strategic risk management, you could enter into a long-term equity derivative contract that pays off only if a chosen market basket of tech stocks goes down. For a known cost up front, you substantially reduce your exposure to a tech stock sell-off that would drag your partner's stock down, but you retain the upside in your partner's stock and you preserve your strategic business relationship with your partner. As CEO, you would decide whether the cost was worth the strategic advantage.

Governments preside over an impressively complicated set of risks. Some of these risks—price supports, credit guarantees, health and welfare entitlements, disaster relief, pension commitments, deposit insurance programs—look like futures and options. These risks should be explicitly recognized and actively managed, not only to prevent large losses to the taxpayer but to reinforce the effectiveness of government programs. The ability to avoid or shed risks that are unnecessary to the success of a program allows more risk to be taken in essential functions. More people can be helped at lower cost. Government can also use risk management techniques to increase the confidence of the public in the soundness of government policies. For example, by issuing puts on government debt (allowing investors to sell their bonds back to the government at a known price) or by being the payor on Consumer Price Index swaps, the government might convince the markets that the government cannot afford to let inflation get out of hand. The U.S. government has taken a step in this direction by issuing inflation-indexed bonds. Increased confidence in the government's commitment to fight inflation will lower the inflation risk premium that is built into bonds and other financial assets, lowering the cost of capital for businesses and individuals throughout the economy and increasing economic growth.

Individuals now face more risk but they also have more choices, such as where and how to invest their nest eggs or which health plan to choose. Good risk management can help them take advantage of new opportunities and make better decisions that improve their chances of being able to live the way they want to live. But there is a big problem. Very, very few individuals are going to have the inclination or ability to become experts in risk management (even those that read this book). They all have day jobs. By necessity, individuals will often need to rely on professional advisors and product suppliers who have risk management skills. Even so, individuals remain on the hook for they will suffer the most from bad advice or flawed products. They must know what to look for in an advisor or supplier and must decide who to trust. They must make sure that their personal beliefs and preferences are taken into account. They must stay on top of what is happening and make changes whenever a relationship appears to be heading off track.

The individual's greater need for sound risk management is not being met as well as it could be. This statement is even true in the financial arena, where risk management has advanced so far. Most people have little enthusiasm for trying to sort through the bewildering array of complex financial products that is pushed at them by financial advisors, banks, brokers, and insurance agents. They don't want to become amateur financiers; they just want to achieve their financial goals and spend their spare time fishing or playing bridge. When you want transportation, you go to a dealer who sells you a fully assembled car that you can drive off the lot. You don't go to the transmission store, the engine store, and the fender store and try to assemble your own car. But today's financial industry expects untrained individuals to design and assemble their own financial security from component parts—without an instruction manual. A financial firm with good risk management capabilities could do much better than that. For example, it could offer a retirement account that offered a lifetime financial safety net with an upside potential. It would guarantee a minimum level of spending power for life but would also offer the chance to participate in gains from financial investments. Imagine knowing that no matter what happened to interest rates, inflation, health care costs, your ability to work, or the stock market, you and your family would always be assured of having at least x percent of your current purchasing power—with a good chance of doing much better than that. The financial firm would produce this product by using its risk management expertise to combine components such as stocks, bonds, life insurance, health insurance, disability insurance, and custom-designed derivatives into an integrated whole.

From your perspective, the product would be simple to understand and might be a very good fit to your risk and return preferences.

THE FUTURE

Even as we try to catch up to the changes in the world that have already occurred, we must look forward to greater change in the future.

Within a few years, we will be operating in a fully wired (or perhaps wireless) global marketplace for goods, services, and financial instruments. The buzz-phrase "anytime, anywhere transactions" will actually be true for most of the things we want to buy or sell. We see this marketplace taking form now on the internet. Communications and transactions will be done securely and privately by advanced cryptography supported by appropriate business contracts and practices (which are not in place on today's internet). You will buy or sell a stock or a bond or a frying pan or a 1 percent interest in Tiger Wood's lifetime earnings and receive instant confirmation and settlement. You will know exactly where you stand at any moment because the current value and composition of your entire net worth will be available on your Palm Pilot (if you don't lose that little pen that comes with it). Events that move markets will move them instantly because everyone paying attention will have the ability to act instantly. Anyone on Earth could be a potential seller if you want to buy and a potential buyer if you want to sell. Vast databases and human experts on every imaginable subject will be tapped at will (the Web has given us a preview of this). Sophisticated analyses will be run to help you make sense of it all.

Genetic engineering will allow you to have customized vegetables and customized children. A baby girl with blonde hair? Blue eyes? IQ of 180? (200 costs too much.) Good tennis player? Dry sense of humor? No problem. What do you want?

Feeling a little blah? Have Drugstore.com FedEx your custom brain cocktail that is mixed just right to get your neurotransmitters back in line. What mood do you want?

What's on TV tonight? Everything (but still nothing).

All these opportunities will be wonderful, but think of the awesome complexity and speed of it all. Think of the risks. So many uncertainties to assess. So many preferences to sort out. So many alternatives and so many decisions to make. So little time to decide. How will you cope?

You will be a good risk manager.

INDEX